A BRIEF HISTORY OF MONEY

For Emma

THIS IS A WELBECK BOOK

First published in 2020 by Welbeck,
an imprint of Welbeck Non-Fiction Limited,
part of the Welbeck Publishing Group
20 Mortimer Street
London W1T 3JW

Design © Welbeck Non-Fiction Limited 2020
Text copyright © Welbeck Non-Fiction Limited 2020

A CIP catalogue for this book is available from the British Library.

ISBN 978-1-78739-445-2

Printed in Dubai

10 9 8 7 6 5 4 3 2 1

A BRIEF HISTORY OF MONEY

4,000 YEARS OF MARKETS, CURRENCIES, DEBT AND CRISIS

DAVID ORRELL

WELBECK

CONTENTS

INTRODUCTION

THIS BOOK IS ABOUT MONEY, THE SUBSTANCE THAT PLAYS SUCH A HUGE ROLE IN OUR LIVES AND YET SEEMS STRANGELY ELUSIVE, NOT JUST BECAUSE IT IS HARD TO OBTAIN, BUT ALSO BECAUSE IT IS HARD EVEN TO DEFINE. WHAT IS IT ABOUT THESE PIECES OF METAL, OR PAPER, OR MORE COMMONLY TODAY JUST NUMBERS IN AN ACCOUNT, THAT EXERT SUCH A HOLD OVER US? AND WHAT GIVES MONEY ITS CONSTANTLY SHAPESHIFTING QUALITY? AS WE'LL SEE, EVERYTHING FROM COWRIE SHELLS FOUND ON A BEACH, TO WOODEN STICKS, TO BITCOINS MINED ON A COMPUTER, HAVE SERVED AS MONEY – SO WHAT IS THE SECRET ESSENCE THAT INFUSES THEM TO GIVE THEM VALUE?

The idea of money seems even harder to pin down when we consider its multiple contradictory properties. For example, those of us who are fortunate enough to live in the developed world have, on average, more wealth and riches than any other period in history – and yet surveys consistently show that money is the leading cause of stress.

We pursue money because we think that obtaining it will make us happy. In the jargon of economists, we are maximizing our utility. And money certainly brings a great deal of joy, which is why people buy lottery tickets. Yet empirical studies show that money only makes us happy to a degree and can actively make us unhappy if we chase it too hard – as shown by increasing rates of depression and suicide in our richest cities. Material wealth and mental health seem to be somehow at odds.

Viewed objectively, what should count is absolute wealth – our net worth – rather than relative wealth, which is how net worth compares to that of other people. Yet most people focus on the latter, and tend to compare themselves with anyone who makes a little more. In 2019, an audience member on a BBC show reacted harshly when it was suggested that his £80,000 salary put him in the top 5 per cent of earners: "I am nowhere near in the top 5 per cent, let me tell you. I'm not even in the top 50 per cent." BBC fact checkers soon showed that £25,000 put you in the top 50 per cent and £81,000 in the top 5 per cent, or globally witin the top 1 per cent. Even when we are rich, it often doesn't feel that way.

Indeed, the more you think about money, the more conflicted it seems. As another example, one of the defining features of money is that it is supposed to be a stable measure of wealth. The dynamics of money, however, are highly volatile, as indicated by the never-ending series of bubbles and crashes which characterize our highly financialised global economy.

Some economists argue that money is not an object at all but is better seen as an abstract idea, which certainly makes sense in our era of virtual fiat currencies. But if that is so, why does it feel like we are handing over a precious object when we make a payment?

Money is supposed to make the concept of value clear and objective so that we can make rational choices, and we often treat it as a rather boring and abstract subject best left to the business section of newspapers. And yet the topic of money arouses powerful emotions, which is why it features in the plots of numerous books and films. Money can bind us together, but it can also break us apart, at the level of people – arguing about money is one of the leading causes of divorce – or at the level of entire countries (see the euro zone crisis).

One might think that economists should be experts on the topic of money but, in fact, it plays a surprisingly

small role in the subject. Mainstream economists have long downplayed or ignored money, treating it only as a metric rather than a thing in itself. One reason the banking crisis of 2007–08 went unpredicted was because the models used by economists did not include banks. As the former Bank of England Governor Mervyn King once noted, "Most economists hold conversations in which the word 'money' hardly appears at all." Like sex or power, money is a force that is rarely discussed out in the open.

This book will unpack this fascinating subject, addressing these numerous questions and concerns by presenting the story of money, from its earliest incarnations some three millennia ago, to the modern financial hubs in cities around the world.

An outline of the book is as follows. Chapter 1 begins with the roots of money as a kind of accounting system in ancient Mesopotamia, and the advent and spread of coin money in ancient Greece and Rome. Chapter 2 shows how money revealed another side during the Middle Ages, when a shortage of metal money was compensated for by an increasing use of virtual instruments such as cheques, bills of exchange, and the first banknotes.

Chapter 3 shows how metal made a spectacular comeback with the European conquest of the New World, and how the gold standard came to underpin the world financial order

for hundreds of years. Chapter 4 discusses the rise of fiat currencies, starting with John Law in early 18th-century Paris, and extending to the Nixon Shock of 1971.

Chapter 5 describes how the field of economics handled – or rather, didn't handle – the topic of money as it developed from the time of Adam Smith, and Chapter 6 investigates how the dynamics of money lead to financial bubbles and crises. Chapter 7 considers cyber currencies and the advent of the cashless society. Finally, Chapter 8 looks at what new approaches to economics such as behavioural economics teach us about money, and what lessons we can learn from its history.

One caveat – money is, of course, a complex and global phenomenon and its history consists of a multitude of different threads. The approach here is to focus on how monetary developments, particularly in the West, have co-evolved with the development of economic thought. The reason, as we'll see, is that our ideas about money both shape, and are shaped by, the prevailing monetary system.

They say that money talks, so this book will listen to what it has to say. We begin the discussion by meeting the people who first invented this extraordinary, volatile, creative, unpredictable, and often dangerous substance – ancient accountants.

• Above: A 19th century Rolling room

PART 01

OLD MONEY

OLD MONEY

WHEN WE THINK ABOUT THE ORIGINS OF MONEY, WE USUALLY IMAGINE THAT IT EMERGED AS A REPLACEMENT FOR BARTER AT SOME POINT IN THE DISTANT PAST. THE STORY GOES BACK AT LEAST TO ARISTOTLE, WHO WROTE IN *POLITICS* THAT THE ADOPTION OF MONEY WAS MAINLY A MATTER OF CONVENIENCE: "THE VARIOUS NECESSARIES OF LIFE ARE NOT EASILY CARRIED ABOUT, AND HENCE MEN AGREED TO EMPLOY IN THEIR DEALINGS WITH EACH OTHER SOMETHING WHICH WAS INTRINSICALLY USEFUL AND EASILY APPLICABLE TO THE PURPOSES OF LIFE, FOR EXAMPLE, IRON, SILVER, AND THE LIKE." THESE MATERIALS, THEREFORE, SERVED AS A MEDIUM OF EXCHANGE. AS A FURTHER CONVENIENCE, "IN PROCESS OF TIME THEY PUT A STAMP UPON IT, TO SAVE THE TROUBLE OF WEIGHING AND TO MARK THE VALUE."

Economists such as Adam Smith later came to a similar conclusion, arguing that money emerged naturally as a substitute for barter. In his 1776 book *Wealth of Nations*, which formed the basis of what is now called classical economics, he fleshed out the picture with descriptions – apparently based on what was known at the time about North American Indians – of hunters and shepherds exchanging "bows and arrows … for cattle or for venison". Again, the role of the state was limited to stamping a value on the metal, so their role was similar to that of "stamp-masters of woolen and linen cloth".

Even modern textbooks, if they discuss the subject at all, usually describe money as having emerged in this manner from barter, often in language which is eerily similar to that of Aristotle. The same is true in popular culture. Director Steven Soderbergh's satirical film *The Laundromat* begins with two white-suited money launderers, played by Gary Oldman and Antonio Banderas, explaining how money emerged from barter as they walk among a group of cavemen. The story does have an appealing sense of logic to it – after all, as the 19th-century economist William Stanley Jevons noted, "A hunter having returned from a successful chase has plenty of game, and may want arms and ammunition to renew the chase. But those who have arms may happen to be well supplied with game, so that no direct exchange is possible." Money was the perfect solution to a practical problem.

"HOW MANY PEOPLE RUIN THEMSELVES BY LAYING OUT MONEY ON TRINKETS OF FRIVOLOUS UTILITY?"
ADAM SMITH

However, this old story cements two ideas about money. One is that money is really no different from any other commodity, except that it is convenient to carry and exchange. The second is that the role of the state is only to come along at the end and put a stamp on the money, as they might put a certificate on a baby seat to certify that it is safe, which is certainly a reassuring feature but not strictly speaking necessary to the functioning of the device. The implication is that money is really nothing special at all.

As we will see in this book, both of these core ideas, which permeate much of our thinking about money, are rather misleading. And money (fortunately) is very special indeed.

• Above: A still from the film *The Laundromat*, directed by Steven Soderbergh. The film is based on the Panama Papers scandal.

• Above and right:
A Hudson Bay
trading token:
One Made Beaver.

ORIGINS

Let's start with the idea that before money, everyone relied on barter. To assess the truth of this statement, ancient philosophers such as Aristotle or, for that matter, modern economics textbooks, probably aren't the best source. If we turn instead to anthropologists, who actually study this kind of thing, it turns out that economies based purely on barter don't appear to exist, or (probably) ever to have existed.

Yes, when indigenous people first encountered Europeans, they frequently engaged in barter. In the 18th century in Canada, the Hudson Bay Company even used a unit of account called the Made Beaver (or MB), which was a male beaver skin, and introduced tokens that were denominated in fractions of MB. But as the 19th-century anthropologist Lewis Henry Morgan observed, trade between people of

the Iroquois nations was handled through longhouses where goods were stored before being allocated by women's councils. In general, barter seems to be a specialized form of trade that occurs between people who are strangers, or even enemies. The word "barter" is from the Old French for "deceive" and was, therefore, associated with the idea of ripping off a potential adversary.

Another case where barter is popular is when people are used to using a monetary system but for some reason the normal currency isn't available, so they have to make do with a substitute. Cigarettes, for example, used to play this role in American prisons, but according to a 2016 study of one prison, ramen soup packages were the currency of choice, which is certainly a healthier option. As one inmate explained, "You can tell how good a man's doing by how many soups he's got in his locker. 'Twenty soups? Oh, that guy's doing good!'" The packages could be used to pay other inmates for services such as cleaning or laundry, or for buying food smuggled from the kitchens. One advantage of cigarettes or ramen is that they are inflation-proof: if their value goes down, they are consumed.

Even in cases such as this where the usual form of money becomes unavailable, it is more common for people to switch to a credit system. Adam Smith wrote that dried cod served as a kind of currency in Newfoundland during the early days of the fishing industry, which certainly seemed to back up the idea that such schemes were destined to be replaced by coin money, if only because gold doesn't smell of fish. What was really happening was that fishers were selling their fish at market price to traders, and getting a credit in return. They then used the credit to purchase supplies. The fishers weren't buying supplies with fish, or engaging in barter, because the money was there all along, in the invisible form of a tab.

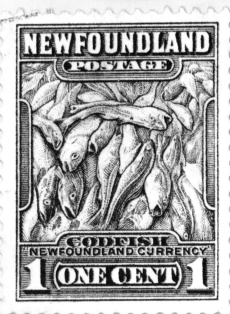

- Top: A bowl of Ramen noodles.
- Above: A 1932 Newfoundland cod postage stamp.
- Opposite, bottom: An Iroquois longhouse in Ontario, Canada.

• Anticlockwise from top: some examples of objects that have been used as currency: cowrie shells, Manilla, dog teeth, wampum shells and paper.

Anthropologists can produce numerous examples of so-called primitive currencies that were based on commodities. Cacao beans in ancient Mexico; cowrie shells in ancient China; tools, iron rings, or brass rods in parts of Africa; human skulls in Sumatra; or woodpecker scalps among the Karok people of the Californian interior. Feathers in the Solomon Islands. Dog teeth in Papua New Guinea, and whale teeth in Fiji. Strings of wampum beads in the American colonies. Extremely large and heavy stone discs in the Pacific island of Yap. And so on. Yet these weren't generally used in the same way as money – a Solomon Islander didn't show up at the corner store with a handful of feathers, and a Yap Islander didn't roll a giant stone. Instead these objects were used as part of social arrangements such as marriage and the settling of disputes.

• Right: These giant yap stones were used as currency in the Western Caroline Islands.

The origin story that money evolved from the use of commodities, like fish or metal or anything else, as a medium of exchange, also implies that the role of the state is only to come along and put a stamp on money. It is true that money doesn't necessarily need government involvement in order to function, as the ongoing existence of cyber currencies such as bitcoin show (we return to this topic later). This view of money, however, also downplays the importance of the stamp. And when it comes to money, the stamp isn't some extra convenience – it's the whole thing.

Consider a US dollar bill. If we ignore for now the portrait of Washington on the front, and the strange things going on with the picture of an eye on top of a pyramid, and another of an eagle, and the various signatures and statements and so on, then the most obvious thing about the bill is the heavy emphasis on the number one. The back of the bill has a written "ONE" and a numerical "1" in each corner. Also "ONE DOLLAR" is written along the bottom, and there is a large "ONE" in the middle. There are also four "1"s and two "ONE"s on the front, giving a total of sixteen reminders that the thing you are looking at is worth exactly one dollar.

In other words, what makes money special is its use of number, so it is unsurprising that money would have been invented by the same people who brought you numbers: the ancient Sumerians.

CLAY MONEY

The Sumerians lived in the area of southern Mesopotamia that lies between the Tigris and Euphrates rivers in what we now call the Middle East. Along with money, the Sumerians also invented writing, arithmetic, the 24-hour day, wheeled vehicles, beer, and the whole concept of urban living. Cities such as Ur, which was located in modern-day Iraq, made up a thriving economy, consisting of tens of thousands of urban dwellers, along with farmers, who kept them supplied with agricultural produce. The cities were ruled by temple bureaucrats, who allocated provisions and tracked commercial transactions using the clay tablets known to ancient historians and museum visitors as cuneiforms.

One of the earliest known examples of human writing is a Sumerian tablet, about 5,000 years old, that shows human heads eating from a bowl, which symbolized rations, along with conical vessels, which meant beer. The tablet was an early version of a ration slip, or perhaps the equivalent of a modern boss taking the staff out for a drink.

Temple accountants indicated weights using a system of units that, like their number system, was based on multiples of 60. Around 3,000 BC they began to use a shekel of silver – which is equivalent to around 8.3 grams, or about what is in a solid silver ring – as a unit of currency. The price of everything else was set by the state in terms of these shekels. The Laws of Eshnunna, named after a city near what is now Baghdad, specified prices for various commodities, where volume was measured in units of sila that corresponded to about a litre:

• Below: A map of Mesopotamia and other parts of the East.

• Above: The Ziggurat of Ur was built over 4,000 years ago in what is now Iraq.

• Below: This Sumerian tablet shows the beer ration for a particular worker.

600 silas of barley (can be purchased) for 1 shekel of silver. 3 silas of fine oil – for 1 shekel of silver. 12 silas of oil – for 1 shekel of silver. 15 silas of lard – for 1 shekel of silver. 40 silas of bitumen – for 1 shekel of silver. 360 shekels of wool – for 1 shekel of silver. 600 silas of salt – for 1 shekel of silver. 300 silas of potash – for 1 shekel of silver. 180 shekels of copper – for 1 shekel of silver. 120 shekels of wrought copper – for 1 shekel of silver.

For comparison, at the time of writing the price ratio for silver to copper is about 80. A month's basic labour was 1 shekel of silver. There was also an early version of Uber:

A wagon together with its oxen and its driver – 100 silas of grain is its hire; if (paid in) silver, ⅓ shekel is its hire; he shall drive it for the entire day.

The document also specified legal penalties for a variety of offences, many of which seemed to involve forms of physical dismemberment:

If a man bites the nose of another man and thus cuts it off, he shall weigh and deliver 60 shekels of silver; an eye – 60 shekels; a tooth – 30 shekels; an ear – 30 shekels; a slap to the cheek – he shall weigh and deliver 10 shekels of silver.

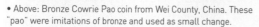

• Above: Bronze Cowrie Pao coin from Wei County, China. These "pao" were imitations of bronze and used as small change.

But, while price lists were set in shekels, this didn't actually mean that people bought things by physically exchanging pieces of silver any more than fishers in Nova Scotia carried pieces of dried fish around in their wallets. Silver did circulate to a degree in its raw form, but it wasn't stamped or shaped into coins. Instead, the shekels were better seen as a unit of account in what amounted to a credit system. For example, a farmer's use of wool or beer could be paid for at harvest time by delivery of the corresponding quantity of barley, as calculated using official prices. Larger debts were recorded on cuneiforms, which were placed inside clay envelopes and marked with the seal of the borrower. The creditor would keep the envelope, and break it open when the debt was repaid, thus canceling the debt. In some cases the tablet promised to repay whoever held the envelope, which meant that the right to collect the debt could be sold on to another person. As we'll see, many forms of money start off as debts in exactly this way.

Loans attracted interest at a rate known as the *máš*, which meant baby calf – money procreated just like farm animals. For commercial loans the basic rate was set at $1/60$ per month, or 20 per cent a year, which could be easily computed since the number system was based on 60.

The invention of money and interest-bearing debt led naturally to the invention of bankruptcy, when people failed to pay those debts. The Sumerian rulers occasionally cancelled all debts in what later came to be known as "Debt Jubilees". Today, the call for debt forgiveness continues with calls to cancel national debts of developing countries, or student loans in the US.

So where was the actual silver that supposedly under-pinned the money system? That was located in closely guarded vaults in the temple but one imagines that in a state run by a single religious authority, few people would have insisted on inquiring into the condition of the reserves. The money was, therefore, more like a virtual currency, where what really counted was the backing of the state. The situation was in some ways similar to that in remote logging or mining camps in the US during the Great Depression in the late 1920s and 1930s, where a portion of wages were paid in company "scrip" that could only be redeemed at the camp's store (which was also the only store), with the difference that in Sumeria the company ran the church as well.

Of course, the Sumerians weren't the only people to come up with the idea of money, but they were the best at documenting it. Ancient Egypt had a system based on weights of grain known as deben. Wheat was deposited in centralized warehouses that were effectively banks. Pre-imperial China employed a number of forms of currency, including cowrie shells, and credit instruments such as notched pieces of bamboo which recorded debts. The first metallic coins to appear in China were imitations in bronze and copper of cowrie shells, and the Chinese character for money 钱 is said to be based on its shape.

To summarize, the Sumerians had a functioning financial system that involved money, debt, taxes, legal penalties, and so on, which was based neither on barter nor on coins. Rather than say that coin money emerged naturally from barter, as the Aristotelian story goes, it would make more sense to say that money was a designed social technology. And in this early form of money – as well as in the money we use today – what counted was not so much the underlying commodity, which was usually nowhere to be seen, but the numbers.

COIN MONEY

The Canadian media theorist Marshall McLuhan once wrote that the reason "money talks" is because "money is a metaphor, a transfer, and a bridge." He also famously wrote that "the medium is the message" and money would find a new voice when it was given a new form: coin. This medium of coin money unleashed the power of money in a way that changed not just the course of history, but even the way we think about and experience the world.

The first known coins date to the 7th century BC, in the kingdom of Lydia (modern-day Turkey). They were discovered during the British Museum excavations of the Temple of Artemis at Ephesus in 1904–05. The coins were

• Left: A modern re-imagining of the Temple of Artemis, one of the Seven Wonders of the ancient world.

• Below: These coins were found on the site of the Temple of Artemis and are thought to be the first Greek currency.

oval pieces of a gold–silver alloy called electrum. They were made by placing a blank round of metal on top of a die, which bore an image like the head of a lion, and hammering it down with a punch.

As Aristotle and later economists pointed out, this new coin money had many advantages as a medium of exchange. As a piece of metal it had an intrinsic value of its own, but at the same time it was easily transportable. It could be accurately weighed and measured, and was certified with a stamp, meaning that it would always be accepted within a certain region. But these coins were not intended for small, everyday transactions, simply because they were worth too much. One stater (a translation of shekel) weighed about 14 grams and would pay about a month's basic salary. Smaller denominations were available down to $\frac{1}{96}$ stater but the most common coin was $\frac{1}{3}$ of a stater, so around ten days' wages.

The Lydians were active traders and while it isn't known how much they used coins for trade, the idea itself certainly spread to nearby areas – first to the Greek cities of coastal Asia Minor, and from there to the mainland and surrounding islands. By 600 BC, most Greek city-states were producing their own coins. Since then, as we will see, power over the money supply, and the right to dictate what is legal tender, have been defining attributes of statehood.

"MONEY IS A METAPHOR, A TRANSFER, AND A BRIDGE."

MARSHALL MCLUHAN

This hints at the real purpose of coin money, which is that it had less to do with the needs of everyday life, than with the needs of the state. Money certainly aided the development of markets but as historian Michael Crawford notes, this was really an "accidental consequence of the coinage". The main application of money – its killer app – was funding expensive wars.

By far the largest expense for states at the time was paying and supplying the army, and coins were a neat way of addressing a number of logistical issues. Troops were paid using metal that was mined or plundered, they spent the

• Above: A silver coin, called a tetradrachm, depicting Alexander the Great.

money on things like food and supplies, and the state then demanded some of the coins back as taxes. The fact that the general public had to get their hands on money in order to pay taxes – for example, by feeding or housing soldiers – solved the logistical problem of how to maintain the army.

In a way, this was just a formalization of a system that was already in place to a degree. Soldiers and mercenaries had long been paid with a share of the spoils of war, and a liquid and easily converted asset like gold was particularly useful when you were travelling (or invading) abroad. The fact that the coins were stamped by the state meant that they had a guaranteed value, at least in areas controlled by the army. And their acceptance was further guaranteed by the fact that suppliers needed to get their hands on the coins to pay taxes. The whole system worked like a kind of game, where the rules were defined by the state and enforced by the military.

The basic unit of currency in ancient Greece was the drachma. The word was from the Greek for grasp or seize, and was a unit of weight referring to a handful of grain. The most popular coin was the silver tetradrachm, which was

equivalent to four drachmae. The coin featured an image of the goddess Athena on one side and an owl, symbolising the wise Athenian people, on the other. These coins contained around 15–20 grams of silver, and would have paid about two weeks of unskilled labour. The silver was extracted from mines such as the ones in Laurium, about 50 kilometres south of Athens, where the pits were worked by some 20,000 slaves.

The system was perfected by a student of Aristotle called Alexander the Great (356–323 BC). During his conquest of the Persian Empire, salaries for his army of over 100,000 soldiers amounted to about half a ton of silver per day. The silver was obtained largely from Persian mines, with the labour supplied by war captives, and was formed into Alexander's own coins. These had an image of the supreme god Zeus on the back, and Hercules on the front.

Alexander would go on to invade the Babylonian empire in Mesopotamia. In a forceable update of their financial technology, he wiped out the existing credit system and insisted that taxes be paid in his own coins.

ANCIENT ROME

Coin money therefore didn't emerge all by itself any more than the Sumerian credit system did. In each case they were imposed by the state. At the same time, money created its

• Above: Another coin depicting Alexander the Great. Currency was a propaganda tool as well as a means of exchange.

own markets and institutions, such as banks and money changers, that grew to have a life of their own. Money also promoted new kinds of social interactions and transactions, and helped to coordinate and control activity, because it gave everyone a clear set of rules. Money changed the way people think by making formal mathematical calculation an important part of everyday life. It is probably no coincidence that the adoption of money coincided in ancient Greece and other parts of the world with a cultural blossoming in science, politics, and the arts.

By the time Alexander died in Babylon at the age of 32 (the cause of death is debated), the area he had conquered included the Middle East, Persia, and Egypt, as well as parts of Afghanistan, Central Asia, and India. Just as military power is responsible for the domination of the US dollar today, Alexander's coins continued to be minted for some 250 years. Because culture often tends to follow the money, coins spread around the world and were stored in libraries like the famous one in the Egyptian city of Alexandria, named after the conquering hero. This is one reason why modern textbooks still teach Aristotle's theory of money.

Alexander was admired by many Roman leaders and generals. Pompey "the Great" received the epithet in emulation of his childhood hero, and he even copied Alexander's distinctive "anastole" haircut where the hair is brushed up from the forehead (or perhaps he didn't like the Julius Caesar bowl-cut, as copied by Facebook's Mark Zuckerberg). And as the Roman Empire grew in power, the Greek invention of coin money helped drive its expansion.

The word "money" originates from the fact that the first coins in Rome were minted in the temple of Juno Moneta, which was named for the goddess who was the protectress of funds. Other mints were set up in the provinces and by the 2nd century BC mobile mints even occasionally accompanied the army, like a kind of cash machine. The government's largest expense was always the army, and the main purpose of the money system was to keep the military machine running smoothly.

Coins were available in gold, silver, and bronze. As always, the stamp did much more than certify the metal content; it also served to define and promote the power of the state. Early coins generally featured traditional Roman images, such as the two-faced god Janus. As time went on the designs became increasingly political, with emperors, magistrates, and even the moneyer adding their names to

• Opposite, top: The Temple of Juno Moneta, as it may have appeared in Rome in 312 AD.

• Opposite below: A Roman silver denarius depicting the great general Pompey.

• Right: A Roman didrachm. The obverse depicts the two-faced god Janus; the reverse shows a four-horse chariot race.

the coins. The coins usually featured a portrait of the stern-gazed reigning emperor on one side, and a propagandist design of some sort on the back.

Larger transactions, such as the purchase of an expensive property, were based on credit. As Cicero wrote, "*nomina facit, negotium conficit*" (provides the bonds, completes the purchase). The bonds (*nomina*) corresponded to entries in account books, which could also be transferred from one person to another, in a kind of proto-bond market. The centre for such financial dealing was the Forum, where money lenders gathered in a passageway known as the Exchange. In an archaic version of a credit-rating system, the names of debtors who defaulted on their loans were inscribed on a column called the Columna Maenia. Private companies known as *publicani* were responsible for tax collection in the provinces, and could also arrange money transfers. If you wanted to send money to some remote outpost in Spain or North Africa, you could deposit money or a bond in the Rome branch, and the funds would be made available for pickup at the other end.

It seems that credit was also available for smaller purchases. In his *Ars Amatoria*, the poet Ovid gives timeless advice to a young man wishing to please a lover who "has her purchase in her eye":

"IF YOU COMPLAIN YOU HAVE NO READY COIN, NO MATTER, 'TIS BUT WRITING OF A LINE; A LITTLE BILL, NOT TO BE PAID AT SIGHT: (NOW CURSE THE TIME WHEN THOU WERT TAUGHT TO WRITE.)"

OVID

RISE AND FALL

The most common Roman coin was the denarius, which was the equivalent of the Greek drachma. The name was from the Latin *deni* for "in tens" because it was worth ten asses, which were smaller coins. Today the name lives on in Italian denaro, Spanish dinero, Portuguese dinheiro, or the dinar currency in several (mostly Islamic) countries.

When the coin, which had a diameter of about 20 mm, was first introduced around 211 BC, it contained about 4.5 grams of near-pure silver, and would pay a day's wages for a soldier or an unskilled labourer. Hundreds of millions of coins were struck. In the mid-2nd century AD alone, imperial spending has been estimated at 225 million denarii per year, with about 75 per cent going to supply the military.

As time went on, emperors got into the habit of recalling the coins, and reissuing with the same face value, but less metal content. The extra silver could then be sold, which was an easy way to make money. Here we see the tension between the two sides of money – the virtual number and the physical object – asserting itself. In ancient Sumeria, the link between the shekel and the silver was mostly theoretical, but in Rome, a soldier always had the option of selling his pay for the silver content, and an emperor could do the same.

• Above: A coin from the reign of Domitian (AD 51–96).

• Below: A coin from the reign of Hadrian (AD 76–138).

Another problem was that, because Rome produced very little itself, money was continuously draining away to foreign lands, a process that only accelerated as Romans consumed increasing quantities of exotic goods from India and China. By the 3rd century AD, the lack of new foreign conquests also meant that the supply of precious metals decreased. Finally, the army was growing increasingly expensive as it ballooned in size to 650,000 in the 4th century, even as the size of the empire itself was shrinking.

The decline of the empire was tracked by the silver content of the denarius, which slowly shrank from an initial 95–98 per cent, to about 50 per cent by the mid-3rd century AD, and then all the way down to about 2 per cent, so that by AD 280 the coin was a piece of copper with a thin coating of silver. The debasement of the coins contributed to extreme inflation, as more of them were issued to pay the state's expenses. During one spell of hyperinflation in AD 274–75 prices multiplied by a factor of 100. The rot was only stopped when the emperor Constantine I introduced the solidus coin in AD 312. This coin contained 4.5 grams of solid gold and was worth 275,000 denarii. The word "soldier" is named after the coin, which certainly highlights the link between coin money and the military. It later became known as the bezant, and remained in production for some seven centuries.

THE TWO SIDES OF MONEY

To summarize the story so far, money did not emerge naturally from barter, but is better described as a designed social technology. It combines within it two contradictory aspects: the concept of a number, and the concept of an owned thing. Sumerian shekels emphasized the number aspect, even if the name referred to a weight of silver, while coin money emphasized the latter, even if the silver on later Roman coins tended to rub off with use. As we'll see, money throughout history has alternated between periods where the virtual side or the real side dominates.

This duality at its core also helps to explain some of the more confounding properties of money, because numbers and owned things have very different properties. Numbers are timeless and obey eternal mathematical laws – the equation $2+2=4$ will always hold true. Owned things, in contrast, tend to age and change with time. The basic incompatibility between numbers and things means that money is intrinsically unstable, and subject to sudden change. In the next chapter, we will see how it made yet another transformation during the Middle Ages.

• Above: A coin from the reign of Constantine (AD 272–337).

VIRTUAL MONEY

THE FALL OF THE ROMAN EMPIRE SAW A DRASTIC REDUCTION IN TRADING ACTIVITIES, MARKETS, AND EVEN THE SIZE OF CITIES, WITH THE POPULATION OF ROME DECLINING FROM AS MANY AS A MILLION IN THE 2ND CENTURY AD, TO ABOUT 30,000 BY AD 550. THE POWER VACUUM WAS FILLED BY THE CHRISTIAN AND ISLAMIC RELIGIOUS AUTHORITIES WHO, INSTEAD OF STAMPING OUT COINS TO PAY SOLDIERS, PREFERRED TO HOARD PRECIOUS METALS IN CHURCHES AND MONASTERIES, OFTEN MELTING IT DOWN AS DECORATION FOR SACRED SYMBOLS.

One result of this transformation – versions of which occurred also in China and India – was that money became increasingly virtual. Like the Sumerian shekel, it was an abstract score-keeping device more than something you could weigh in your hand. And once again, the birthplace of this next monetary revolution was in Mesopotamia – with the difference that this time it was led by Islamic money lenders. As today, Islamic finance did not allow usury, but did permit profit-sharing, or charging a range of fees. The system relied heavily on credit instruments, including the promissory notes known as *sakk*, or "cheques". The fact that such transactions were backed only by a signature meant that in business a person's reputation or credibility (from the Latin *credere* for believe or trust) was all-important.

"ALL MONEY IS A MATTER OF BELIEF."

ADAM SMITH, ATTRIBUTED

As seen in the previous chapter, the invention of money was closely tied to the invention of numbers. It is therefore unsurprising that this developing credit system coincided with the mathematical discovery of negative numbers (a concept which will be familiar to anyone who has overextended their credit card). The first explanation of how to work with both negative numbers, and the number zero was given in the 7th century by the Indian mathematician Brahmagupta, whose book *The Opening of the Universe*

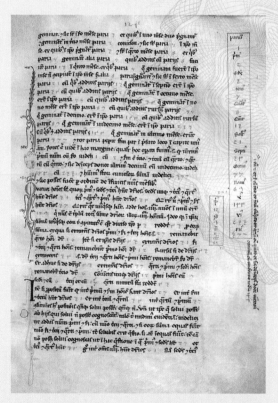

• Opposite: A manuscript by Leonardo Fibonacci, who helped popularize what has come to be known as the Arabic number system.

• Above: A page from Luca Pacioli's *Summa de* arithmetica. Pacioli was one of the pioneers of double-entry book-keeping.

was written entirely in verse. He called positive numbers "fortunes" and negative numbers "debts", which made the connection with money clear. Zero was the unique number whose negative is itself (he didn't invent the concept, but he did show how to use it in equations). Translations of his book spread these concepts through the Islamic world, where the number zero was incorporated in the Arabic number system. From there, word spread to Europe through the Moorish conquest of Spain.

The use of the Arabic number system was popularized by the Italian mathematician Leonardo Fibonacci (1170–1250), who learned the Arabic system as a child while growing up in Bugia (now in Algeria). In his 1202 book *Liber Abaci* (*Book of Calculation*) he showed how calculations such as division or multiplication were far easier using Arabic numbers than they were with the Roman system. Many of the examples involved financial activities such as money-changing, the calculation of interest, book-keeping, and so

on, and the book soon found an audience with merchants.

The Arabic number system received a less enthusiastic reception from the Church and the state, who worried about the ease with which a number like 3 could be modified to look like an 8. Or perhaps it was the "not invented here" syndrome at work. In 1299 the government of Florence even banned its use. Merchants, however, continued to use the system in ciphered messages – the word cipher, meaning code, is from the Arabic *sifr* for zero – and the concept of negative numbers was key to the development of double-entry book-keeping, which was later codified by the mathematician Luca Pacioli in his 1494 book *Summa de arithmetica*. The technique was so named because every transaction was entered in two different accounts, once as a debit and once as a credit. The sum of all debits should therefore equal the sum of all credits, just as a positive number and its negative add to zero, which was useful for detecting errors.

FEUDALISM

During the Middle Ages, Christian Europe operated under a feudal system, which was strictly hierarchical. The ultimate authority was the sovereign, who granted land to lords, who granted plots to vassals, who did all the grunt work such as farming the land and fighting in wars. Estates were relatively closed and self-contained communities, in which rents and taxes were paid in terms of produce or labour rather than through coin. The most powerful landlord was the Church, which also dominated the thinking about economic matters. Usury was forbidden, and the pursuit of wealth for its own sake was a capital sin.

Most coins used in everyday small transactions were made of copper and were of low value. The denier, denoted "d" and named after the Roman denarius, was a more valuable silver coin. Twelve deniers made up one sou, and twenty sous made up a livre (lira in Italy), which was theoretically worth a pound of silver. Both the sou and the livre, however, were just abstract units of account, and 240 deniers made up rather less than a pound of silver (a French denier for example only weighed 1.2 grams). The British version of the denier was the penny, denoted in the same way by the symbol "d". Instead of a sou, 12 pennies made up one shilling, and instead of a livre, 20 shillings made up a pound sterling. This system remained in place until decimalization in 1971.

More valuable coins were also minted for major transactions such as international trade. The Florentine florin, for example, contained 3.5 grams of gold and was struck from 1252 to 1533 with no major change either to its design or to its metal content. The design featured the

• Left, top and middle: A coin issued under the reign of Edward the Confessor (1042–1066).

• Left: A gold florin issued in 1486 in the Republic of Florence.

fleur-de-lis badge of the city on one side, and on the other a depiction of St John the Baptist wearing a hair shirt, which probably deterred people from making trivial purchases. The similarly sized Venetian ducat (duke's coin) was introduced in 1284. Both coins had numerous local versions – the Dutch guilder which was abbreviated to Fl. after florin – and ducats were still in use until the early 20th century.

As in ancient Rome, sovereigns frequently couldn't resist treating their own coinage as a source of precious metal to be plundered. France alone debased its currency on average about once every two years in the 14th and 15th centuries – which might explain why we use the French word seigniorage to describe the process of making money by issuing currency. One such intervention by Philip VI in 1349 was responsible for about 70 per cent of his total takings.

A more upfront form of the same thing was the practice known as recoinage, where coins were only valid for a certain period, and had to be periodically returned and exchanged for new coins, for a fee. In England around the end of the 10th century, coins were recalled every six years, and replaced with new ones at the rate of three new for four old. The seigniorage amounted to 25 per cent every six years. In a number of northern European countries, including Germany, Austria, and Scandinavia, the main coin type during the 12th and 13th centuries was the *bracteate*. These circulated only in a small area, such as a town or region, and were made of a wafer-thin sheet of silver, stamped on one side over a soft surface so that the negative appeared on the other. They didn't last long, but that was no problem

• Right: Ducats issued by the Republic of Venice.

• Top, left: A coin issued by Harald I Bluetooth of Denmark (10th century).

• Top, right: Silvio Gessell, an early socialist.

• Above: A coin issued in the 12th century by the German Ascanian dynasty.

because they were recalled as often as twice a year, with annualized seigniorage rates as high as 50 per cent or more.

Recoinage wasn't very popular among non-sovereigns, for obvious reasons, but one advantage was that it didn't introduce inflation, which remained very low in Europe during this period. The seigniorage earned from recoinage is today called a Gesell tax, after the German economist Silvio Gesell, who argued that the practice – which is equivalent to a kind of negative interest rate – encourages spending and boosts the economy. As he wrote in 1913, "Only money that goes out of date like a newspaper, rots like potatoes, rusts like iron, evaporates like ether, is capable of standing the test as an instrument for the exchange of potatoes, newspapers, iron and ether. For such money is not preferred to goods either by the purchaser or the seller … we must make money worse as a commodity if we wish to make it better as a medium of exchange."

WOODEN MONEY

Some of the alternative currency schemes discussed later incorporate a similar form of negative interest. For example, the air miles issued by airlines often become invalid if they aren't used before a certain period. The fact that the issuer of money also has control over its spending power is a reminder once again of the tension that exists between the two sides of money, the virtual number and the real object. The dual nature of money was made explicit in the beginning of the 12th century, when King Henry I of England introduced a payment system that was based on wooden sticks.

The sticks, known as tallies, were made of polished hazel or willow wood, and were initially used to record a debt. The stick was first notched to indicate the numerical value of the debt. The code was described in a 12th-century treatise called *The Dialogue Concerning the Exchequer*: "At the top of the tally a cut is made, the thickness of the palm of the hand, to represent a thousand pounds; then a hundred pounds by a cut the breadth of a thumb; twenty pounds, the breadth of the little finger; a single pound, the width of a swollen barleycorn; a shilling rather narrower; then a penny is marked by a single cut without removing any wood."

The tally was then split lengthwise down the middle so that each side carried a matching record of the amount. The creditor kept one part known as the stock (from which we get "stockmarket"), which was slightly longer. The debtor got the other part, known as the stub, from which we derive "getting the short end of the stick". When the debt was retired, the (positive) stock would be matched with the (negative) stub, and the tally destroyed (since a positive plus its negative equals zero). The sticks were more durable than parchment, and people didn't need to be literate to understand them. The result was therefore a medieval version of Sumerian cuneiforms, with wood instead of clay.

The tallies were used by the exchequer as a tool for collecting taxes for some seven centuries, but they also circulated as a form of money in their own right. For example, suppose the state held a stock representing a debt owed to it from a local tax sheriff. Rather than wait for the tax sheriff to pay up, it could use the stock to pay a supplier. The supplier could then collect later from the tax sheriff, or alternatively use it to pay their own taxes, or even sell the stock at a discount to a broker who would collect the debt when it came due. A similar system existed during the Middle Ages in China, with the difference that the tallies were made of bamboo.

Tallies remained in use in England until 1826. In 1834, the remaining sticks were collected up and burned in a stove under the House of Lords but the fire ran out of control and burned down the building. The extant Palace of Westminster was built in its place.

• Below: A wooden tally stick used for tax purposes.

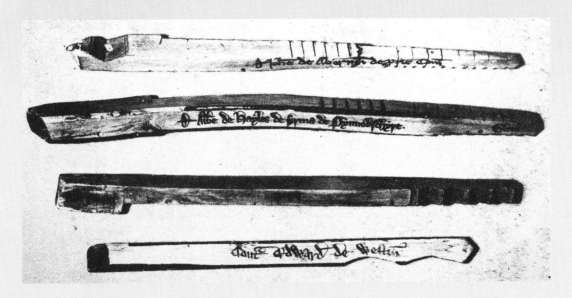

Another form of virtual money in the Middle Ages was an early version of traveller's cheques, which was established by the secretive, ascetic, warrior order of monks known as the Knights Templar. A widespread belief is that the knights discovered and kept religious artefacts including the Holy Grail. Even if they didn't, they certainly appear to have discovered the Holy Grail of making money.

During the 12th and 13th centuries, a major preoccupation of European powers was to capture Jerusalem from the Muslims. A pilgrim or soldier who was about to set off on the Crusades could deposit some funds at a participating castle, in return for a letter of credit which they could use to withdraw money at other branches along the route. While

• Above: The Houses of Parliament destroyed by fire. 16 October 1834

• Opposite: The burning of Jacques de Molay, Grand Master of the Knights Templar.

usury was forbidden, the Knights Templar made money by other means, such as taking a cut of the rent on a property while its owner was away. At its peak, the organization had about 870 branches and employed about 7,000 people but their wealth brought them enemies. After they cut off the indebted French King Philip IV from further loans, he cracked down on the knights, sentencing their leaders to death by burning, and confiscating their immense riches.

BILLS OF EXCHANGE

When the Venetian explorer Marco Polo returned from China in 1295, he brought word of a new kind of virtual money. His book *The Travels of Marco Polo* described the strange system, administered by the government of Kublai Khan, in which people accepted money that was made from sheets of paper, signed and stamped with the royal seal: "All these pieces of paper are issued with as much solemnity and authority as if they were of pure gold or silver … everybody takes them readily, for wheresoever a person may go throughout the Great Kaan's dominions he shall find these pieces of paper current, and shall be able to transact all sales and purchases of goods by means of them just as well as if they were coins of pure gold." The scheme obviously worked, since the Chinese economy was doing well at the time, and an appealing feature from the perspective of the state was that it could hang on to its real gold and silver instead of releasing it as currency.

European bankers and goldsmiths soon copied this example, on a smaller scale, by issuing paper promissory notes in exchange for deposits, that were payable to anyone who had them in their possession. These pieces of paper were known as *nota di banco*, from which the word "banknote" derives. The next major leap in financial technology was a kind of private money known as the bill of exchange.

In an era when international trade was blossoming, coin money had a number of problems. Coins were often in bad shape after being "clipped" which referred to the practice of shaving a small amount of metal from the edges. In 1529, when Francis I of France paid 12 million escudos to ransom his two sons who had been substituted for him as hostages after his capture, it took the Spanish four months to count and test the coins, and 40,000 coins

• Above: A page from *The Travels of Marco Polo*, published in the 13th century.

"I HAVE NOT TOLD HALF OF WHAT I SAW."

MARCO POLO

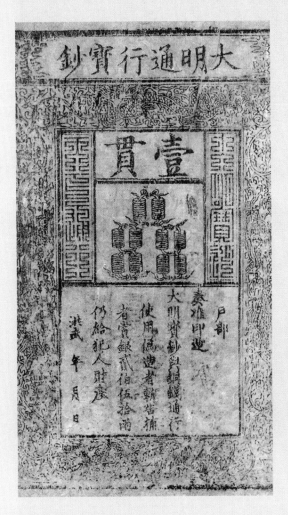

• Above: The oldest existing banknote, issued in the 14th century by the Ming dynasty.

were rejected. Coins were also rather impractical for foreign transactions. Should a merchant in Florence want to import goods from a Parisian supplier, the merchant could, in theory, physically carry the money to France and change the coins for local currency. One problem was that this was slow – the transportation might take a few months. It was also dangerous, since robberies were common. Finally, exchanging the currency at the other end incurred more expenses.

Merchants, therefore, adopted an instrument known as a bill of exchange. This was a document that instructed a banker or agent to make a payment on the writer's behalf. The merchant could purchase a bill of exchange from a bank in Florence that allowed him to withdraw the same amount, at a set exchange rate, from a bank or agent in Paris. Unlike cheques, which didn't appear in Europe until the late 14th century, bills of exchange could only be cashed or deposited in person.

The amount of the bill was usually denominated in virtual units of account such as sous, or the imaginary unit known as the *écu de marc*. This had two set exchange rates, one for the local currency used at purchase, and one of the currency at the destination. Included in the exchange rates was a commission covering the banker's fee.

The system was similar to the Knights Templar scheme, with the difference that it was used not only by the rich and powerful, but also by a broad class of merchants. International trade fairs, which were becoming increasingly popular in towns such as Lyon, where one was held quarterly, were also becoming increasingly cashless. When the trading was complete, bankers would gather together, agree on exchange rates, cancel out the various payments, and settle outstanding balances using bills of exchange.

USURY

While bills of exchange helped grease the wheels of trade, they could also be used for other things. For example, bills provided a way to speculate on currency trading, which could be highly lucrative. Indeed, one of the main advantages of bills of exchange was exactly that, like modern cyber currencies, they offered an alternative to the official state system, which was a useful feature at a time when exchange rates were fluctuating due to wars or devaluations. Bills of exchange could also be used as a way to borrow money. If someone needed a pay-day loan they could sell a bill, drawn on themselves, which would be payable at the next fair. The commission on such a loan amounted to an effective interest rate of 2 to 3 per cent per quarter.

For Christians, usury was officially forbidden because it was considered to be a form of avarice, which was a mortal sin. It was also seen as a form of theft, because usury made money out of time, and time belonged only to God. (This restriction didn't apply to Jews, which is one reason that Jewish communities became centres for the burgeoning financial services sector.) The Church's view of usury was in part based on that of Aristotle, whose ideas were being promoted in the universities being established in places such as Bologna (founded in 1088), Paris (c. 1150), and Oxford (1167). According to Aristotle, monetary profit of any kind amounted to theft: "The most hated sort, and with the greatest reason, is usury, which makes a gain out of money itself, and not from the natural object of it. For money was intended to be used in exchange, but not to increase at interest. And this term interest, which means the birth of money from money, is applied to the breeding of money because the offspring resembles the parent. Wherefore of all modes of getting wealth this is the most unnatural."

One benefit of this view of time and interest was that when it came to big projects, such as cathedrals, time wasn't an issue. Many towns such as Amiens took out massive loans to finance their buildings, and construction could go on for centuries. Modern governments, who are more acutely sensitive to the time value of money, would be loath to take on such projects, yet ancient cathedrals are among the most enduring monuments in Europe, and in financial terms continue to boost their local economies through things like tourism.

As the economy and the role of money grew in size, however, a debate began in the new universities and elsewhere about whether usury was as bad as all that. After all, the interest on a loan could be viewed as compensation for the risk that the loan would not be repaid, or for the fact that the money could not be put to another use. Therefore, while the Church continued to condemn usury, society in general became more relaxed about it. One loophole was that a lender could require that the debtor pay insurance against default.

The link between time and money was also made more concrete by the invention and development of mechanical clocks. These were initially used to prompt bell-ringers in monasteries and cathedrals but were soon put to use in regulating the work day and, eventually, every other aspect of people's lives. Benjamin Franklin later wrote in his 1748 "Advice to a Young Tradesman" to "Remember that Time is Money" since someone who "can earn Ten Shillings a Day by his Labour" but takes half the day off to relax or enjoy himself "has really spent or rather thrown away Five Shillings".

• Opposite: A 17th-century Dutch painting depicting an old woman weighing gold.

"TIME IS MONEY."

BENJAMIN FRANKLIN, "ADVICE TO A YOUNG TRADESMAN"

• Above: Money changers depicted in this celebrated painting
by Quentin Massis (1514).

• Opposite: Amiens Cathedral.

THE MEDICIS

As the European economy grew in size, it also grew in complexity. Manufacturers set up specialized guilds, and business people formed organizations that later became known as companies. Money lenders and changers established their own guild called the Arte de Cambio, and joined forces to create the first banks and insurance companies. The centre for innovation in what is today known as financial technology, or "fintech", was the northern trading cities of Italy such as Venice, Genoa, and Florence, which had become wealthy through trade with Asia. These new institutions lent money to a wide range of people including landlords, vendors, and merchants like the fictional Antonio in Shakespeare's *The Merchant of Venice*.

The growth of commerce also coincided in some countries with a decline in the feudal system. In England, for example,

• Above: Genoese bankers depicted in this 15th-century manuscript.

• Opposite: Cosimo de Medici, Lord of Florence, one of the most powerful bankers in medieval Europe.

the privatization process known as enclosure meant that tenants were increasingly evicted from common land. Rather than live on their estates, feudal lords increasingly preferred to live as *rentiers* in cities such as Paris, while investing their capital in businesses or other assets. States became more centralized under strong monarchs, and chivalric knights were replaced with professional armies who clashed in increasingly costly wars.

Economic growth went into sudden reverse with the arrival in the mid-1300s of the Black Death, which caused the deaths of an estimated one-third of the European population. However, the demand for labourers after the plague outbreak had subsided meant that wages rose and living standards generally increased. Social mobility increased as the power of the nobility and the Church declined. And the power of money was unleashed with the development of a new class of financiers, led by the Medici family.

The Medici Bank was founded in 1397 by Giovanni di Bicci de' Medici, who did well enough that when he died in 1429 he left a fortune worth some 180,000 gold florins. In terms of gold content, that amounts to about $30 million at today's price. Things really took off under his son Cosimo, who oversaw an expansion through the major cities of Europe. His wealth made Cosimo de Medici into the de facto ruler of Florence, and together with his grandson Lorenzo he commissioned buildings and artworks which made the city the tourist attraction that it is today.

After Cosimo's death in 1464, the Medici Bank began to fall into decline. One factor was the family's spending habit, which Lorenzo estimated, for the period 1434 to 1471, to be an average of almost 18,000 gold florins a year. According to the political philosopher Niccolò Machiavelli, the bank started calling in loans for repayment, which caused a number of Florentine businesses to collapse, and led to a plot against Medici rule.

It was a former clerk at the Medici Bank in Florence called Amerigo Vespucci who would both lend his name to a new continent, and inadvertently play a key role in the next phase of monetary development.

• Opposite: Botticelli's *Adoration of the Magi* (1475). Cosimo de Medici is depicted as the Magus kneeling before the Virgin, and other members of the Medici family are depicted in the scene.

REAL MONEY

AS WE HAVE SEEN SO FAR, MONEY BEGAN AS A VIRTUAL CREDIT SYSTEM IN ANCIENT MESOPOTAMIA, FLIPPED TO A METAL-BASED SYSTEM IN ANCIENT GREECE AND ROME, AND THEN REASSERTED ITS VIRTUAL SIDE THROUGH INSTRUMENTS SUCH AS CHEQUES, TALLIES, AND BILLS OF EXCHANGE IN THE MIDDLE AGES. JUST AS THE EARTH SWAPS ITS MAGNETIC POLARITY ON AVERAGE ABOUT TWICE EVERY MILLION YEARS, IT SEEMS THAT MONEY CHANGES ITS POLARITY ABOUT ONCE OR TWICE EVERY MILLENNIUM.

The trigger for money's next move was the discovery of vast amounts of very real metal in the New World. As Amerigo Vespucci wrote in a 1503 letter to his patron, Lorenzo de' Medici, "... it is lawful to call it a new world, because none of these countries were known to our ancestors and to all who hear about them they will be entirely new." The letter was published with the Latin title of *Mundus Novus* (*New World*), but they soon came up with a better name – America.

Columbus had already made some initial voyages, but thought the land he had seen was part of Asia. The news that it was actually a brand new continent was exciting to the explorers' backers in Europe, and set off a wave of exploration.

Of course, America wasn't really new at all, and it actually played host to advanced civilizations such as the Mayans, Incas, and Aztecs who had developed their own systems of agriculture, writing, mathematics, law, religion, trade, and so on. In some ways these systems were similar to the European versions, but one key difference was in the approach to metals such as silver and gold. Perhaps because these were in plentiful supply, the locals valued them for their beauty and religious significance, but not so much for commerce. The Incas thought that gold represented the sweat of the sun and silver the tears of the moon. They used the metals to line their temples, rather than buy things at the store – which rather contradicted the longstanding story that the use of coin money emerged naturally as some kind of inevitable historical process.

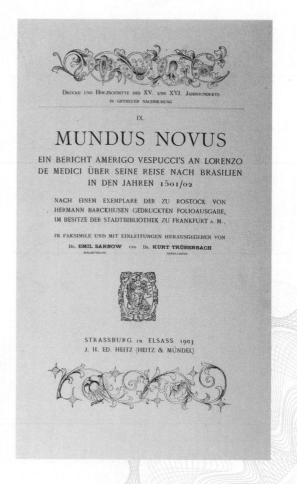

In fact, the Incas seemed to get along without any kind of money at all. Instead, in what seems like an advanced form of feudalism, distribution was handled by the government. According to the anthropologist Gordon McEwan, "Each citizen of the empire was issued the necessities of life out of the state storehouses, including food, tools, raw materials, and clothing, and needed to purchase nothing. With no shops or markets, there was no need for a standard currency or money, and there was nowhere to spend money or purchase or trade for necessities." Anyone who has been on a cruise where the restaurant menus have no price list will know the same feeling, with the difference that, of course, cruise passengers pay for all the meals in advance.

The Aztecs had a highly superior version of a money system which was based on cacao beans. Rather like the prison currencies discussed in the introduction, these beans had the advantage that if they were not required for small purchases, they could be dried, roasted, and used to make a very bitter-tasting drink. The Europeans later added sugar, and called it chocolate.

• Opposite: *Mundus Novus* by Amerigo Vespucci, where he describes his voyage to the New World.

• Above: Machu Picchu in Peru.

FEATHERED SERPENT

The first major clash between the new and old worlds occurred in 1519, when the Spanish conquistador Hernán Cortés and his army of several hundred arrived in Mexico. After a few stops and skirmishes with the natives along the coast, Cortés reached what is now Veracruz. In order to eliminate any possibility of retreat, he ordered his men to scuttle their ships.

There are two versions of what then happened. According to the Spanish version, the rulers of Yucatán had predicted the appearance of a blonde, bearded deity known as Quetzalcoatl, or Feathered Serpent. When Cortés arrived with his blonde hair and beard, the Aztecs believed their vision had come true, greeting him not like the invading enemy he was, but as a god.

The Aztec view was completely different, one suspects, but that version of the story has, unfortunately, been lost

to history. Either way, the emperor Moctezuma II allowed Cortés and his men to enter the capital Tenochtitlan, which was home to over 200,000 people, and presented him with lavish gifts of gold and silver.

If the intention was to encourage Cortés to go away, the emperor's show of generosity had the opposite effect. Instead, what happened was that Cortés decided to find out if there was any more where that came from. His men were similarly affected by the sight of precious metal. As the Franciscan friar and missionary priest Bernardino de Sahagún described, "They picked it up and fingered it like monkeys. It was as if their hearts were satisfied, brightened, calmed. For in truth they thirsted mightily for gold; they stuffed themselves with it; they starved for it; they lusted for it like pigs." Even Cortés himself wondered if his soldiers were stricken by a "disease of the heart which can only be cured by gold".

The lust for gold ended only with the death of Moctezuma, the sacking of Tenochtitlan, and eventually the conquest of the entire continent. The fight would not have been so one-sided, were it not for the fact that the Spanish invaders carried with them a different kind of disease, namely smallpox. The Aztecs had no immunity – a quarter of their population is estimated to have died in the ensuing epidemic. The impact of the disease on the Incas was even more harsh. The disease swept through their entire society within months, killing the emperor and much of the rest of the population. Millions of the indigenous population also died working in gold and silver mines, where health and safety regulations were notably absent. Accidents such as rock falls and cave-ins, or exposure to the mercury used in the refining process, or sheer exhaustion, took a horrible toll.

Author Mark Cocker wrote, "When viewed as a single process, the European consumption of tribal society could be said to represent the greatest, most persistent act of human destructiveness ever recorded." And it was all in the name of money.

• Opposite: Hernán Cortés meeting the emperor Moctezuma.

• Below: The Fall of Tenochtitlan in 1521, when the Aztec empire was extinguished.

THE RESOURCE CURSE

It was certainly a lot of money. In the three centuries from 1500 to 1800, American mines produced about 150,000 tons of silver and 2,800 tons of gold, which was most of the world's supply. The mountain in Peru known as Cerro Rico (rich hill) alone produced some 45,000 tons of pure silver. It is still being mined by the locals on a smaller scale today, but is now in danger of total collapse. In the Portuguese colony of Brazil, gold production amounted to more than 16 tons a year, with labour supplied from about 150,000 (mostly African) slaves.

The pattern resembled that set by the ancient Greeks and Romans – invade new territory, put slaves to work in mines, coin the metal to finance the operation – but on a far larger scale. Some of this silver ended up in what is considered to be the first international coin: the Spanish dollar. Also known as the piece of eight, or the peso, the dollar was a silver coin of approximately 38 mm diameter, that was worth eight Spanish reales. It was first minted in Spain in 1497, and then in Mexico and Peru, but versions

"IN THE STATES WHICH MAKE USE OF DEGRADED MONEY, REIGNS COWARDICE, LAZINESS AND INDOLENCE."

NICOLAES COPERNICUS, *MONETAE CUDENDAE RATIO*

soon spread around the world. The coin eventually served as the basis for the United States dollar, the Canadian dollar, the Chinese yuan (from the word for "round things" which referred to Spanish dollar coins) and the Japanese yen (an abbreviation). The name "dollar" actually comes though from the Czech mining town of Joachimsthal, near the German border (it is now more of a spa town). Silver coins minted from the area were known as Joachimstals, which was later shortened to thalers or talers, and pronounced in English as "dollars".

Somewhat ironically, the flood of freshly minted dollars in Spain, and the world economy as a whole, didn't translate into quite the economic boom that one might expect. Even most conquistadors made little money – they were responsible for paying their own expenses, and the crown charged hefty taxes on any takings. Cortés himself ended up broke following a failed venture in California. Some of the treasure was lost to pirates on the way back to Europe, or to the oceans following shipwrecks. What did make it back tended to end up in the hands of the state and nobility, who, like the Aztecs, seemed to value it mostly for its ornamental use, gold-plating their palaces, coaches, books, and so on. And the gold and silver that wasn't so used mostly left the country through trade, often on rather poor terms.

China, in particular, had a huge demand for silver. Its innovative experiment with paper currency had wound down after bouts of hyperinflation, and it was back on hard money. The economy was also booming with the opening of new trade routes. By the late 16th century, China was importing almost 50 tons of silver a year in exchange for

• Right, top and middle: Silver Spanish dollars from the 15th century.

• Right, below: A silver thaler from 16th-century Germany.

• Opposite: Cerro Rico in Peru, which has produced at least 45,000 tons of silver.

goods such as silk and porcelain (often called china in English because it usually came from there). Gold was imported as well, but it was valued for its beauty rather than being used as money.

The biggest beneficiaries of New World wealth were, therefore, not the explorers or their Old World funders, but the merchant bankers from Italy, Holland, and Germany who facilitated the Asia trade and acted as middlemen. At the same time, inflation meant that the cost of living in Spain went up, and trade was affected as Spanish goods became relatively expensive compared to foreign goods.

The dangers of inflation were explained by the astronomer Copernicus in a 1526 treatise called *Monetae cudendae ratio* (*On the Minting of Coin*). As he wrote: "Innumerable though the evils are with which kingdoms, principalities and republics are troubled, there are four which in my opinion outweigh all others – war, death, famine, and debasement of money ... in the States which make use of degraded money, reigns cowardice, laziness and indolence." The main problem was one of money supply, since "money usually depreciates when it becomes too abundant."

The influx of New World metal also resulted in what is today known as the resource curse, where a dependence on natural resources degrades other aspects of the economy, and leaves the country vulnerable to any drying up of its supply. In Spain, gold shipments peaked in the mid-1500s, silver a few decades later. The country became a net debtor, and between 1550 and 1700 defaulted on its debt 14 times. Decline was accelerated by costly military ventures such as the failed invasion of England by the Spanish Armada in 1588. The sugar rush of the money boom wore off without much in the way of long-term benefits – a problem with which policy makers continue to wrestle today as they balance the costs and benefits of monetary stimulus.

• Opposite: The great astronomer Nicolaus Copernicus, who was much concerned with the debasement of currency.

• Right: A so-called Dragon Dollar from China, 1889.

MERCANTILISM

In Spain, a group of contrarian economic thinkers known as the Arbitristas (in English, the arbitrators) argued that the economic decline of Spain in the 16th century was because people had grown lazy on speculation and easy money, which also led to widening social inequality. Or, as one member of the group, Gonzalez de Cellorigo, put it in 1600, "Spain is poor because she is rich." Most economists (the term had not yet been invented) in other countries, however, continued to be distracted by the obvious appeal of shiny pieces of metal and developed a theory of economics, later known as mercantilism, that measured a nation's power by its ability to accumulate treasure. Underlying this approach was the monetary theory known as bullionism, which assumes that the value of money is due solely to its weight in precious metal.

A leader in this area was England under Queen Elizabeth I, which made up for its lack of native resources through the time-honoured tactic of taking them from other countries. As with the Spanish conquistadors, the process was largely delegated to private companies. The largest was the British East India Company, which was founded in 1600 with a royal charter for trade monopolies. It was structured as a joint-stock company whose shares were owned by wealthy investors. The company grew into a quasi-military organization that handled half of the world's trade and virtually ruled India with its private armies for a century, even minting its own coinage which became the Indian standard.

One of the company's directors was Thomas Mun (1571–1641), who became a leading exponent of the mercantilist doctrine. The economy was a zero-sum game, so as Mun put it, "One man's loss is another man's gain." The role of the state was to use its military power to keep the resources flowing in and to improve the terms of trade through tariffs, monopolies, and subsidies, with the aim always being "to sell more to strangers yearly than we consume of theirs in Value". Or as Jean-Baptiste Colbert, who served as the minister of finances of France under King Louis XIV, said: "It is simply, and solely, the abundance of money within a

• Top: A Dutch East India Company gold coin from the 18th century.

• Above: The key work by Thomas Mun, a leading advocate of Mercantilism.

• Opposite: An official of the East India Company, c. 1760.

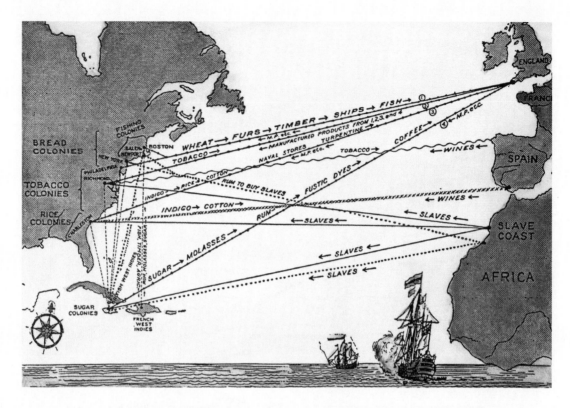

state that makes the difference in its grandeur and power."

What we today call "corporate ethics" was not high on the list of priorities, given that the main trading pattern at the time was a triangular arrangement in which goods such as weapons and textiles were sent from Britain to West Africa where they were swapped for African slaves who were taken under barborous conditions to the Americas. The slaves were exchanged for commodities such as sugar, cotton, and tobacco, which returned with the ships to Europe.

Adam Smith later wrote that the doctrine of mercantilism taught nations that "their interest lies in beggaring all their neighbours". Of course, mercantilism hasn't gone away, and countries including the US and China are sometimes accused of pursuing beggar-thy-neighbour trade policies.

THE CREDIT ECONOMY

During the 17th century, the shortage of coin in countries including England meant that most trade had to be carried out on the basis of credit. People relied on instruments such as sales credit, bills of exchange, bonds and pledges, with the coin system serving as the unit of account and the means of final payment.

The increasing sophistication of the financial sector meant that a variety of other options were available, at least for wealthy clients. People could invest in a range of instruments such as company shares or government bonds. Since 1609, the Amsterdam Exchange Bank had allowed merchants to set up accounts and transfer money, and therefore carry out transactions on paper without needing to handle money directly. And people could also deposit coins and bullion with goldsmiths and notaries, in exchange for receipts, that could be transferred over to someone else as a payment. These instruments all ultimately pointed to some real store of wealth somewhere, but as they proliferated it sometimes became hard to know where exactly that wealth lay.

For example, suppose that a deposit of gold was made with a goldsmith. Since gold is a fungible commodity, where what counts is the weight, the goldsmith just had to make sure that he had enough gold in stock in case the depositor wanted their gold back – it didn't have to be exactly the same gold. Leaving the gold alone in the vault doing nothing was rather a waste, so goldsmiths got into the habit of loaning out some of the gold in order to earn interest on the loan. Or, better yet, they could just loan a receipt for the gold, in the form of a note which gave the bearer the right to withdraw the gold. The note could be used to pay someone, who might use it to withdraw the gold, but that person might also use it to pay someone else, and so on.

Because these loans attracted interest, the goldsmith could afford to pay interest on deposits, which encouraged more deposits and more loans and so on. At the same time, the lines were blurred between the goldsmith's accounts, and what he actually had as physical gold. As Sir Dudley North observed, "merchants kept their money with Goldsmiths and Scriveners [notaries or legal clerics], whose accounts show Ten thousand cash, but they seldom have a thousand in specie."

As discussed later, this was the start of the so-called fractional reserve system in banking. Such loans were not on a large enough scale, however, to improve the money supply

and under the English legal system only the initial creditor could sue the debtor, which discouraged debt instruments from circulating as money. Credit was person-to-person, and didn't scale up. And while richer people could borrow at reasonable rates, poor people had to pay interest rates of 40 to 60 per cent. Economic activity was being stifled by the lack of an adequate monetary system.

A number of schemes were suggested with the aim of fixing this problem by making it easier for people to access credit. Many of these were directly inspired by a rather older method of creating an infinite supply of gold – alchemy.

• Opposite: The triangular trade between Britain, America and its colonies.

• Below: A 15th-century view of a goldsmith's shop.

THE PHILOSOPHER'S STONE

Alchemy was viewed at the time as being a legitimate subject of study. Charles II (1630–1685) built a private alchemical laboratory under his bedroom, and the quest for a philosopher's stone, which could transmute a base metal such as mercury into gold, was taken seriously.

In particular, a group known as the Hartlibians, which formed around the "intelligencer" (e.g. an intellectual figure) Samuel Hartlib, and included practising alchemists, saw credit as a kind of financial philosopher's stone. One pamphlet by William Potter was called *The Key of Wealth: Or, A New Way for Improving of Trade* where "the key" referred to the alchemical knowledge of how to transmute matter. Henry Robinson, a Hartlibian, described his own scheme for a merchant bank as "capable of multiplying the stock of the Nation, for as much as concernes trading *in Infinitum*: In breife, it is the *Elixir or Philosopher's Stone*". The physician Peter Chamberlen, who argued that public property should be converted to stock, called it "the best Elixir: The Philosophers stone".

The basic idea was that the "base metal" of things like land or goods or future earnings could be converted into the "gold" of money through the magic of credit. Suppose someone had a valuable plot of land, but needed access to money in order to pursue a business venture. One approach would be to sell the land, but they may not want to, and even if they did it would probably take a long time. A better method would be to borrow against the land. The creditor would then have to wait to be repaid. If the business venture failed, then the creditor would have a claim against the land, and the owner would be forced to sell. With this method,

no new money would be created, since it would simply be transferred from the creditor to the debtor.

If the creditor instead received notes, however, and these notes could be exchanged, then they would be as good as money. The creditor could then spend them imediately (i.e. pass the debt on to someone else), and the money supply would expand accordingly. As William Potter wrote, this credit currency would unlock society's "store-house of Riches" making credit "the true Seed of Riches". He estimated that the scheme could double England's capital every two years, so after 20 years, £1,000 would grow to £1 million.

Another advantage of credit money was that it was much easier to handle and transport than coin money. Of course, such a scheme would only work if people had complete faith in the credit money thus created. The system needed to be transparent, the managers had to be people of the highest reputation. and enforcement had to be strict and unforgiving, with counterfeiters sent to the gallows.

Some critics worried that creating such a source of infinite credit would lead to runaway inflation, just as discovering an actual philosopher's stone would mean that after a while people would value gold no more than they did mercury. As discussed later, this kind of inflation is a very real concern.

A number of "land banks" along these lines were attempted, but didn't manage to attract enough broad interest to survive. The problem was eventually cracked by a group who found a way to monetize, not their own land, but – at least in a sense – the state itself. The catalyst for the idea was a military defeat.

"THERE IS ANOTHER ALCHEMY, OPERATIVE AND PRACTICAL, WHICH TEACHES HOW TO MAKE THE NOBLE METALS."

ROGER BACON

THE BANK OF ENGLAND

The Nine Years' War of 1688 to 1697 between France, led by Louis XIV, and a coalition of European countries, is considered to be the first global military conflict, given that it stretched geographically from Europe to North America to India. France's greatest naval victory during the conflict was the Battle of Beachy Head (near Eastbourne), on 10 July 1690, in which their force crushed its Anglo-Dutch opponents. The English loss caused panic in the country and acted as the impetus for England to rebuild as a naval power, which required money – around £1.2 million. King William III, also known as William of Orange, was born Dutch and would have been aware of state banks like the ones in Holland or Sweden. The solution involved a variation on that theme, in the form of a public–private partnership.

The Bank of England, as it was called, was, in effect, a very large goldsmith. The money was raised by selling a subscription to private investors. The bank then lent the money to the government, in exchange for tallies. They also received 8 per cent interest in perpetuity on the original loan, plus a service charge of £4,000 per year, plus any fees for banking services. Oh, and also the right to issue banknotes.

Actually, the bank's original charter didn't mention banknotes, but they turned out to be the most important part of the arrangement. At first, like other banks or goldsmiths, the new corporation gave handwritten notes in return for deposits. These notes included a promise to pay the bearer the sum of the note on demand, so anyone could redeem them in full or in part for coins.

One difference was that these notes had royal approval, which meant they were widely accepted. Another more subtle but very important difference was that, instead of representing a debt owed *to* the crown, the notes now represented a debt owed *by* the crown. This change in the polarity of debt marked a switch from money that was purely public, to money that was better seen as a melding of the state with private business. The state handled the virtual stamp, while the private sector handled the real wealth. In a time when royals frequently defaulted or debased their currency, the involvement of the private sector added a new sense of stability and reliability.

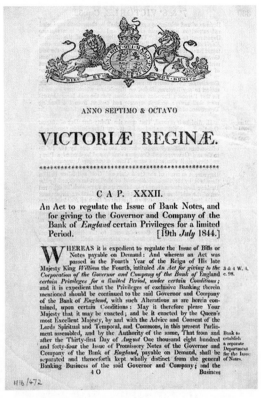

● Above: The charter of the Bank of England.

The bank was originally sited in a small office in the City of London, the square mile that lies within what used to be the Roman town of Londinium. Archaeologists later discovered on the site the remains of a Roman temple of Mithras, the God of Contracts, which seemed appropriate. In 1734 the bank moved to its current location in Threadneedle Street, where it became known as the Old Lady of Threadneedle Street. The complicated relationship between bank and the crown was symbolized by the historic quasi-independence of the City of London – even today the City has its own lord mayor, with whom the ruling monarch needs to check in before entering.

The bank soon established a near monopoly (and in 1844 a full monopoly) in the issuance of notes. It also acted as a clearing house to settle transactions between other banks such as London & Westminster, Lloyds and Barclays, and ultimately became what the financial journalist Walter Bagehot (1826–1877) called the "lender of last resort", responsible for bailing out smaller banks that became the victim of bank runs or other financial crises.

The success of the bank at serving as the central node of the financial system meant that it became a model for other central banks around the world. The economist John Kenneth Galbraith later wrote that the Bank of England "is in all respects to money as St. Peter's is to the Faith. And the reputation is deserved, for most of the art as well as much of the mystery associated with the management of money originated there."

• Below: The Bank of England building today on Threadneedle Street, London.

• Opposite: The Battle of Beachy Head in 1690, which paved the way for the establishment of the Bank of England.

THE SILVER CRISIS

The development of paper money represented the start of another shift back towards virtual money. At the time it didn't challenge the predominant idea that money amounted to a weight of metal, because it was understood that banknotes were just a receipt for the real money – the gold bars and coins – that existed in a vault somewhere. The exact size of the reserves, which consisted of both bullion and government securities, was kept as vague by the corporation as it probably was in ancient Sumeria – part of what Galbraith called the art and mystery of banking. As one essayist recorded some two centuries after the Bank of England was founded:

> Lord Cunliffe, giving evidence before a Royal Commission, at the special request of the Chancellor of the Exchequer, would only say that the Bank of England reserves were "very, very considerable". When pressed to give even an approximate figure, he replied that he would be "very, very reluctant" to add to what he had said.

The association of money with metal was illustrated by the "silver crisis" which afflicted England in the 1690s. At the time England operated under a bimetallic regime, with a mix of low-denomination silver and high-denomination gold coins. A problem inherit to such arrangements is that the relative value of the coins had to reflect accurately the market exchange rate between the two metals, since otherwise the undervalued coins tended to be melted down or sold abroad as bullion. For several decades, this had been the fate of many silver coins, whose face value was a few per cent less than their worth as metal. The widespread practice of clipping the coins and selling the valuable metal meant that the silver coins that remained contained as little as half their original metal. Merchants therefore discounted the coins, which resulted in inflation, undercutting confidence in the money supply and even the government itself.

In 1694, the government decided that something had to be done, so they issued new coins. A debate broke out over whether the coins should be restored to their former level of silver, or kept at a lower level. Mercantilist economists favoured the latter option since it amounted to debasing the currency, which was always good for trade. Arguing on the other side was the philosopher John Locke, who believed that money's "intrinsic value" was measured by its precious

metal content, and you could no more change it than you could "lengthen a foot by dividing it into Fifteen parts, instead of Twelve".

Locke won the argument, and the silver coins were restored to their former level of content, but this time with milled edges to discourage clipping. An unexpected result was that people hoarded the new silver coins and spent the old ones – an example of "Gresham's law" (named after the 16th century financier Sir Thomas Gresham, though Copernicus had already made the same observation) which states that "bad money drives out good". The shortage of money created severe deflation that was only ameliorated by the increased use of banknotes.

NEWTONIAN MONEY

Locke was acting as an advisor to Isaac Newton, who, at the relatively advanced age of 53, had been offered a sinecure as Warden (later Master) of the Mint. Newton took his position seriously, reorganizing the Mint and applying his alchemical knowledge of metallurgy to the production of coins. He also devoted considerable energy to chasing down clippers and counterfeiters, some of whom were put to death. But his main job was controlling the money supply.

The Mint's flagship coin, and the country's first gold coin to be struck by machine instead of by hand, was the guinea. This coin was named for the region of West Africa where the material was sourced. It contained about a quarter ounce of gold, and was decorated with an image of a small elephant, which was the logo of the Africa Company. In theory it was worth one pound sterling, or 20 silver shillings. In practice, the actual market exchange rate could be rather higher.

In 1717, Newton investigated the matter and concluded that in England, "a pound weight of fine gold is worth fifteen pounds weight six ounces seventeen pennyweight &

• Above: Rightly regarded as perhaps the greatest scientist who ever lived, Isaac Newton spent over three decades working for the Royal Mint.

• Above: A gold guinea coin.

£3.17s.10½d. an ounce, which made a guinea 21 shillings, and turned a weight of gold into the defining unit of the monetary system – even though the unit of value actually referred to a weight of silver. It was as if Newton, who himself had spent years doing alchemical experiments in his laboratory, had succeeded in transmuting silver into gold (or perhaps it was the other way round). The price of gold remained effectively the same until the outbreak of the First World War, some two centuries later, with the only exception being during the Napoleonic wars from 1797 to 1821.

In 1817, a new coin called the sovereign was introduced, which contained $^{20}/_{21}$ of the gold in a guinea, thus making it worth exactly one pound sterling. It seems strange today to think that at the time these coins, which would be valuable collector's items today, were popular coins that circulated widely. The coins are still legal tender, though they are struck only as bullion coins or for collectors (and they are worth a lot more than one pound).

A formal gold standard was established in Britain in 1821, and this soon became an international standard, spreading to the (then) Province of Canada in 1854, Newfoundland in 1865, and the United States and Germany in 1873. The United States used the eagle as its unit, Germany the new gold mark, while Canada hedged its bets and adopted a dual system based on both the British sovereign and the American eagle (much as their spelling today is a mix of British and American).

In the United States, the Coinage Act of 1792 had

five grains of fine silver, reckoning a Guinea at 1£, 1s. 6d. in silver money" (one pound, one shilling, and six pence). He recommended that the price of a guinea be set to one pound and one shilling, or 21 shillings.

In the eyes of traders, this price was still a little low, with the result that, in another example of the law that "bad money drives out good", merchants used silver coins to pay for imports, resulting in a shortage of silver. Newton assumed that the market price of gold would eventually fall as it became relatively abundant compared to silver, bringing prices back to equilibrium – but, as usual, money

"PRECIOUS METALS ALONE ARE MONEY. PAPER NOTES ARE MONEY BECAUSE THEY ARE REPRESENTATIONS OF METALLIC MONEY."

BARON OVERSTONE

had a mind of its own. Instead of the price of gold adjusting, what happened was that the market price of gold (measured in pounds sterling) stayed the same, so guineas retained their face value of 21 shillings, while the price of silver adjusted to a degree but remained volatile.

It seemed that the attractive, machine-made, valuable gold coins had more pull over the monetary system than the shopworn silver coins. The Mint set the price of gold at

originally defined a dollar to be equal to the value of the widely used Spanish silver dollar, which was 371.25 grains of silver, where a grain was $^1/_{7000}$ of a pound (the unit originally referred to a grain of barley). The gold eagles were valued at ten dollars and contained 247.5 grains of gold. The gold/silver price ratio was therefore exactly 15. But when the country later moved onto the international gold standard, the mint stopped coining the silver dollar, resulting in a drastic shrinking of the money supply, which especially affected less wealthy people without access to gold. In a famous 1896 address, the populist politician William Jennings Bryan described the policy as an attempt to "crucify mankind upon a cross of gold".

The debate is also believed to have inspired the themes behind L. Frank Baum's 1900 children's novel *The Wonderful Wizard of Oz*. The Wicked Witches of the East and West represented the rich bankers who wanted to keep on the yellow brick road (i.e. gold). The Scarecrow stood for indebted farmers who wanted a cheaper silver currency, but was helped by neither the Tin Woodsman (industrialists) nor the Cowardly Lion (politicians). The Wonderful Wizard at the central bank made sure that the dollar was measured in ounces (oz) of gold. And Dorothy's red slippers? In the original book, they were silver.

BADGE OF HONOUR

The international gold standard, which Newton inadvertently initiated, was one of the longest-running financial institutions in history. It was successful exactly because, being based like an economic law of gravity on an equation between value and mass, it was global and easily shared, so everyone knew where they stood. The sense of stability it granted was captured by the Austrian writer Stefan Zweig in his autobiography *The World of Yesterday* (1942), in which he wrote how "the Austrian crown circulated in bright gold pieces, an assurance of its immutability. Everything had its norm, its definite measure and weight." The economist Joseph Schumpeter described a country's adherence to the gold standard as a "badge of honor and decency".

The gold standard was not just an abstract mechanism for controlling the money supply, but captured an entire belief system about the meaning of value. According to the 19th century politician Baron Overstone, "Precious metals alone are money. Paper notes are money because they are representations of metallic money." Or as the American banker J.P. Morgan testified in 1912, "Money is gold, and nothing else."

While the gold standard helped protect the currency from the vagaries of politicians, however, linking the quantity of money to a finite commodity also meant that the money

• Banking magnate J.P. Morgan, whose bank thrives to this day. Morgan was self-conscious about his deformed nose and threatened to sue anyone who published unflattering photographs.

supply did not adjust appropriately to the size of the economy and left it vulnerable to changes in gold supply. After a large find or improvement in mining technology, the money supply might become too large, causing inflation. Alternatively, it might not keep up with the pace of economic growth – or with spending – with the result that gold became too expensive, causing deflation and recession. As seen in the next chapter, these restrictions, along with the growing acceptance of banknotes. eventually triggered money's next reversal, as it switched back once again to its virtual roots.

PART 02

NEW MONEY

LET THERE BE MONEY

AT THE SAME TIME THAT NEWTON WAS PUTTING ENGLAND ONTO THE GOLD STANDARD (BY ACCIDENT), A DIFFERENT KIND OF MONETARY EXPERIMENT WAS TAKING PLACE ON THE OTHER SIDE OF THE ENGLISH CHANNEL, HEADED THIS TIME BY AN EX-PAT SCOTTISH MATHEMATICIAN BY THE NAME OF JOHN LAW. WHILE THE RESULTS OF THE EXPERIMENT WERE GENERALLY CONSIDERED TO BE NOTHING SHORT OF DISASTROUS, THE BASIC IDEA – THAT MONEY CAN BE CREATED OUT OF NOTHING – IS WHAT UNDERPINS, IF THAT IS THE WORD, OUR MODERN FIAT CURRENCY SYSTEM.

Law was the son of a goldsmith, a trained mathematician, and something of a rogue. In 1694, at the age of 23, he killed another man in a duel held in Bloomsbury Square, London. Sentenced to death, he somehow escaped custody (money and connections may have helped) and travelled to Holland. There he took up with a married aristocrat, had two children with her, and travelled around Europe supporting his family by gambling. He also put a lot of thought into the topic of money, inspired, no doubt, by the financial innovations taking place in cities like Amsterdam and London.

"I AM A HUMAN BEING. I HAVE MADE GREAT ERRORS."

JOHN LAW

Law returned to Scotland, which at the time had a separate legal system from that of England, and pitched an idea on which he had been working to the Scottish government. In his 1705 text *Money and Trade Consider'd with a Proposal for Supplying the Nation with Money*, he argued that Scotland needed a central bank of its own, similar to the Bank of England, but instead of backing its paper money with metal, it should back it with land, which he argued was the ultimate source of all wealth. The idea was, therefore, similar to the land banks proposed in England by the Hartlibians.

Scotland at the time was in a poor financial state, thanks in no small part to the so-called Darien Venture, in which Scottish colonists tried to establish a settlement called New Caledonia on the coast of the Isthmus of Panama. The venture was led by William Paterson, who had assisted in founding the Bank of England. Investors were confident and in 1698 a fleet of five ships set sail carrying 1,200 people, and what amounted to half the capital in Scotland. Unfortunately that particular piece of land turned out to be an inhospitable mix of jungle and swamp, protected both by disease-carrying mosquitos and local residents, and within seven months the surviving colonists returned home. Meanwhile two other ships had already set out and met

• Opposite: John Law helped precipitate one of the biggest financial scandals in history.

• Above: William Paterson helped establish the colony of New Caledonia in Panama.

a similar fate. The result was described by historian John Prebble as "perhaps the worst disaster in Scotland's history".

Law's scheme was turned down by the government, which instead decided on union with England. This was doubly bad for Law: financial union meant that the financial system came under the purview of the Bank of England, and legal union meant that he would be wanted for murder in his home country. He left again for Europe – where he would eventually find another opportunity to try out his ideas.

THE SYSTEM

As he toured the gambling salons of Europe, Law made many aristocratic acquaintances including the French Duc d'Orleans, who introduced him to the minister of finance Nicolas Desmarets. France was another country in a perilous financial state, thanks in part to the prolific spending habits of Louis XIV (aka the "Sun King") whose home-improvement projects included the palace at Versailles. Law explained his monetary system to the minister, who took it directly to the king, who immediately rejected it.

Law resumed his wanderings across Europe, where his success at gambling – he claimed that he had a "system" – made him a wealthy man. But when Louis XIV died in 1715, Law saw the opportunity to give his monetary theory another shot. He travelled to France and got back in touch with the Duc d'Orleans, who was now acting as regent to the young Louis XV. The regent was convinced, but as usual Law's radical ideas ran into resistance from others, so Law had to make do with permission to set up a small private bank on condition that he financed it himself.

Law's bank worked at first on a similar principle to other banks like the one in Amsterdam, by issuing bank notes against coin deposits. It was very successful just because banknotes were easier to handle than coins, and also couldn't be clipped. In 1718 the bank was nationalized, becoming the Banque Royale, which meant that the notes now had the official backing of the state.

Taking another page from the Dutch playbook, Law also established the Mississippi Company. This had exclusive trading rights over the enormous Mississippi River area, which stretched some 3,000 miles from the mouth of the river to parts of Canada, and included the present-day states of Louisiana, Mississippi, Arkansas, Missouri, Illinois, Iowa, Wisconsin, and Minnesota. Like the Dutch East India Company, the company's stocks could be bought using credit issued by the bank. The prospectus was backed by what amounted to a highly effective real estate marketing plan, which portrayed the region as a kind of El Dorado.

Finally, Law enacted the key part of his monetary theory, which was to announce that the banknotes would be delinked from reserves of precious metals, turning the money into a fiat currency (from the Latin for "let it be done"). Few people, however, paid attention to the technical point of bank reserves, and interest instead focused on the Mississippi Company, whose share price soared due to rumours of huge deposits of gold.

● Opposite: King Louis XIV's prodigal spending habits left him relying heavily on money lenders.

● Below: Early French paper currency, issued in 1720.

> ## "FEAR AND EUPHORIA ARE DOMINANT FORCES, AND FEAR IS MANY MULTIPLES THE SIZE OF EUPHORIA. BUBBLES GO UP VERY SLOWLY AS EUPHORIA BUILDS. THEN FEAR HITS, AND IT COMES DOWN VERY SHARPLY."
>
> **ALAN GREENSPAN**

• Above: It was believed in the 1720s that the Mississippi region contained large reserves of gold.

INFINITE CREDIT

A positive feedback loop was established where bank lending boosted share prices which increased optimism and spending in the economy, leading to more lending and so on – much as the Harlibians had predicted. People flocked from all over the country and abroad to take part in the economic miracle. In 1719 alone, the company share price vaulted from 500 livres to over 10,000 livres, and the word "millionaire" came into use for the first time. It seemed that the financial philosopher's stone had finally been discovered.

As discussed later, the dynamics of financial bubbles have remained the same throughout history. In the space of a few years, this particular bubble turned Law into the richest man in the world. It also released any restraints on his bounding ambitions. In no time he was arranging for the company to buy the national debt, and have the right to collect taxes. This required issuing many more shares, and many more paper notes to buy them with – which is when Law's system started to reveal its flaws.

At the time, tax collection in France was a lucrative activity carried out by tax farmers, and Law's decision to move into the area created powerful enemies. And unlike the Bank of England, which was founded as a public–private partnership, his scheme involved the crown but gave the business and private banking community no direct role except as competitors. Stories appeared that the Mississippi region, as large as it was, might not actually contain any gold, and people started to complain about galloping inflation.

The fall, when it came, was even quicker than the rise. A crash in the shares was accompanied by a run on the bank. Law was exiled to spend his final days in Venice.

Law's story is believed to have inspired Part II of Goethe's *Doctor Faustus*, where Faust and Mephistopheles help a cash-strapped emperor by introducing him to the miracles of fiat currency, supposedly backed by underground reserves of gold. "And people value this the same as honest gold? The court and army take it as full pay? Much as I find it strange, I see I must accept it," says the emperor. Of course it doesn't end well. Goethe's (and Law's) tale remains as relevant as ever, acting as a reminder of the fragile link that exists between money and value – and of the tendency for the money system to suddenly crash without warning.

BURNING MONEY

Law's experiment gave banks such a bad name in France that until the late 19th century, financial institutions avoided the term and prefered to call themselves a *caisse*, *crédit*, *comptoir*, or *société*. However, his ideas landed on more fertile soil in America.

Like France, the American colonies suffered from a shortage of precious metals with which to make coins. The mercantilist overlords in London also forbade the export of gold or silver to other countries, even their own colonies. The main coin in use was the Spanish dollar, but many of these ended up being exported in return for goods. Consequently, settlers often had to rely on commodity money, such as tobacco or wampum beads, with the imperial system of pounds, shillings and pence acting as a common unit of account.

As a result, by the early 18th century a number of colonial governments were experimenting with paper money, primarily for financing expensive projects like military ventures. In 1723 Pennsylvania initiated a scheme that resembled Law's idea for a land bank, in which paper money was backed by future taxes, and the land assets of people who borrowed from the government. One of its main promoters was a Pennsylvania printer by the name of Benjamin Franklin, who at the age of 23 self-published a pamphlet entitled *A Modest Enquiry into the Nature and Necessity of a Paper-Currency*. Franklin had read Law's work, and argued like him that trade depended on a ready and dependable supply of money, which was impossible if

"INFLATION IS THE ONE FORM OF TAXATION THAT CAN BE IMPOSED WITHOUT LEGISLATION."

MILTON FRIEDMAN

the material used to make that money was controlled by other countries.

While the new paper currency was widely seen as a success, the British government took a dimmer view. It passed laws declaring the money illegal and, of course, only accepted gold and silver as payment for tax. The resulting contraction in the money supply led to unemployment which was one cause of the American Revolutionary War (1775–83). As soon as the colonies cut their legal ties with Britain they began to issue their own paper notes to pay for the war, with symbols of the English crown replaced by patriotic emblems.

These notes were printed on thick, handmade rag paper, and often contained watermarks or design details to prevent counterfeiting. One such feature, devised by Benjamin Franklin, involved a thin, lead cast of a real leaf, that was attached to the printing press in order to produce a design that was nearly impossible to counterfeit – much like the wood grain of medieval tallies.

In 1775, Congress passed a resolution to print a single currency known as the Continental that would be used to pay war debts. While they served this task, so many of the notes were printed that they also depreciated over the course of the war from a value of one silver dollar to more like one cent. It didn't help that the British were producing their own counterfeit notes. As Benjamin Franklin later observed, the depreciation was, in effect, a tax that helped pay for the war. "This currency, as we manage it, is a wonderful Machine. It performs its Office when we issue it; it pays and clothes Troops, and provides Victuals and Ammunition; and when we are obliged to issue a Quantity excessive, it pays itself off by Depreciation."

In an attempt to stem inflation, at the end of the war hundreds of millions of dollars were recalled and destroyed, either by punching a hole in the bill or by burning. Today burning money is the specialty of performance artists, but at one time it was official policy.

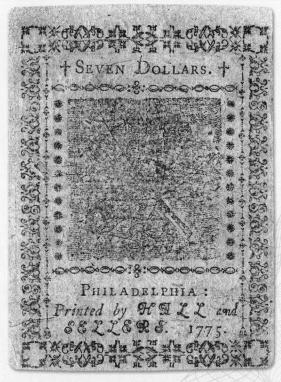

• Opposite, left: A $55 bill, issued in 1779.

• Opposite, right: Among his other achievements, Benjamin Franklin devised a way of preventing counterfeit banknotes.

• Above/Below: A $7 bill, issued by the Continental government in 1775.

HODGES'
Genuine Bank Notes
—OF—
AMERICA.

THE ONLY ORIGINAL AND CORRECT WORK EVER PUBLISHED, EXCEPT THE

BANK NOTE SAFE-GUARD,

GIVING PLAIN, SUCCINCT, AND

RELIABLE DESCRIPTIONS

—OF—

EVERY GENUINE BANK NOTE OF EVERY DENOMINATION ON EVERY BANK

—IN THE—

UNITED STATES & CANADA.

A VALUABLE

DETECTER OF SPURIOUS, ALTERED, AND COUNTERFEIT MONEY,

Compiled carefully from original sources, arranged and published for the use of, and sent without charge, to the Subscribers of Hodges' Journal of Finance and Bank Reporter,

—BY—

J. TYLER HODGES, Banker,

(Author, Proprietor and Publisher of Hodges' Bank Note Safe-Guard; Hodges' Journal of Finance and Reporter, and Hodges' Gold and Siver Coin Chart Manual, &c., &c., &c.)

No. 271 BROADWAY, NEW-YORK.

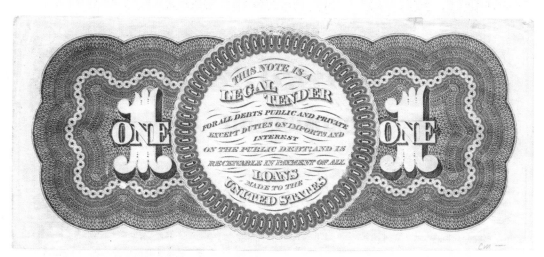

THE DEEPER MYSTERY

Just as Law's bank put the French off banks, so the Continental episode put Americans off paper money – for a while. Rather than issue more fiat currency, Treasury Secretary Alexander Hamilton decided to imitate the Bank of England by setting up a Bank of the United States, and selling shares to the private sector. The scheme suffered more resistance than it had in England, however, and when the bank's 20-year charter ran out, Congress failed to renew. A second attempted Bank of the United States lasted an even shorter time, from 1816 to 1833.

More popular were small private banks, led by a multitude of John Laws, each with their own currency. In 1859,

Hodges' Genuine Bank Notes of America could list over a thousand such banks, and nearly ten times as many kinds of notes. Counterfeiting, needless to say, was big business.

In 1862, President Lincoln tried to bring some order into the chaos, and help fund the Civil War, by signing into law the First Legal Tender Act. This authorized United States Notes – or greenbacks as they became known – as legal tender. Because these notes were not backed by gold or

• Above: Small American banks were free to issue their own banknotes.

•Opposite: The first greenbacks were issued in 1862 to finance the US Civil War.

silver, they did not add to the national debt, or earn interest, but were valid for any transaction apart from paying custom duties. The government also introduced an income tax and excise taxes, which helped mute their inflationary effect.

As Lincoln told the Senate in 1865: "The government should create, issue and circulate all the currency and credit needed to satisfy the spending power of the government and the buying power of the consumers ... Money will cease to be master and become servant of humanity." He was assassinated just a few weeks later, and the greenbacks in circulation were gradually phased out after the war (though they remained legal tender as late as 1971).

The monetary system in the United States remained in a relatively disorganized state until, following a number of financial crises such as the "Panic of 1907", when the New York Stock Exchange declined almost 50 per cent from its previous peak, the Federal Reserve was set up with the cooperation of financiers in 1913. Like the Bank of England, it acted as a central hub for the banking system. Its dollar bills were similar in appearance to the greenback, but were a form of debt money, since they represented a loan from the quasi-private Federal Reserve.

• Top: A view of Wall Street in 1907.

• Above: The US Federal Reserve official seal.

• Opposite: The Federal Reserve building as it appears today. The Fed has sole responsibility for issuing banknotes.

As with many things in finance – such as "quantitative easing" – the Federal Reserve (aka the Fed) is confusingly named. The institution is not part of the federal government, and if there is a reserve it is not clear where exactly it is. In fact the Fed is an independent not-for-profit corporation consisting of 12 regional Federal Reserve banks, each of which is in turn owned by a consortium of commercial banks. According to the Fed's own website, "The Federal Reserve System is not 'owned' by anyone." Yet it is clear that the power resides with the consortium of commercial banks, given that they get to vote on and participate in the Fed's banking operations.

The arrangement is an example of what Galbraith called the "deeper mystery" that seems to be deliberately cultivated around the financial system, and which was epitomized by

the former Fed Chairman Alan Greenspan who reportedly said once that, "If I have made myself clear then you have misunderstood me."

THE NIXON SHOCK

Just a year after the Fed was founded in 1913, the outbreak of the First World War led to suspension of the international gold standard. Following the war, a number of countries tried to resurrect the system. Gold coinage mostly disappeared from use, but gold bullion still served for transactions between central banks. The gold system, however, was showing its flaws. In 1925, Winston Churchill, who was then the UK finance minister, decided to restore the gold price to its pre-war level, resulting in deflation that led to recession and the General Strike.

"WE ARE NOT SPENDING THE FEDERAL GOVERNMENT'S MONEY. WE ARE SPENDING THE TAXPAYER'S MONEY."

RICHARD NIXON

Adherence to the gold standard is also cited as a factor in the Great Depression in the United States, since it prevented the government from boosting the money supply in response. In 1933, President Roosevelt found an innovative way of mining the metal, which was to build a new depository in Fort Knox, and give all citizens three weeks to hand in their gold (apart from a $100 allowance for things like jewellery) in return for cash. The global economic contraction which accompanied the Great Depression led to a rise in political extremism, the rise of the Nazis in Germany, and the outbreak of war.

As the Second World War drew to a close, a conference was held in Bretton Woods, New Hampshire, US, in which representatives from all 44 Allied nations gathered to decide how the international monetary and financial order would be regulated. The meeting was dominated by the US, which was in a much stronger position than its indebted allies. The result was a watered-down version of the gold standard, in which exchange rates between currencies were fixed, and dollars earned through international trade could be redeemed for gold bars at a rate of $35 per ounce. The US,

therefore, essentially controlled the world money supply.

It was only a matter of time before the problems associated with the inflexibility of metal-based currencies reasserted themselves once again. In the early 1960s, international trade was out-growing the money supply, and the US government was also printing money to fund ventures such as the Vietnam War, which had an estimated total cost of over $100 billion, the Apollo space programme ($24 billion), and the Cold War with Russia ($ trillions). In response, the price for gold in private markets began to push above its designated level of $35. In December 1968, with Richard Nixon preparing to take office as president, the economist Milton Friedman wrote a letter urging him to abandon Bretton Woods and allow the dollar to float freely against other currencies.

• Above: The Bretton Woods conference in 1944 set the financial foundations for the post-war world.

• Opposite: The Federal Reserve has a unique public and private structure and is the central monetary institution of the United States.

Friedman had specified that Nixon should move quickly, so he could say the decision was necessary because of the "complete mismanagement by the prior administration of both domestic and international financial policies". However, it took until 15 August 1971 for Nixon to impose a number of measures, including the halting of the dollar's direct convertibility to gold, in an event that became known as the "Nixon shock".

In his televison address, Nixon stated that the American dollar was a "hostage in the hands of international speculators ... We will press for the necessary reforms to set up an urgently needed new international monetary system ... I am taking one further step to protect the dollar, to improve our balance of payments, and to increase jobs for America." That one step was a 10 per cent tax on imported goods. To reassure his audience, he also addressed "the bugaboo of what is called devaluation. If you want to buy a foreign car or take a trip abroad, market conditions may cause your dollar to buy slightly less. But if you are among the overwhelming majority of Americans who buy American-made products in America, your dollar will be worth just as much tomorrow as it is today. The effect of this action, in other words, will be to stabilize the dollar."

Nixon wasn't known as "Tricky Dick" for nothing, because by November of that year the price of gold had reached $100. The Bretton Woods currency system soon ended, and exchange rates between major currencies were allowed to float freely, just as Friedman had said they should. And, as discussed below, all currencies are now "hostage in the hands of international speculators" to use Nixon's phrase.

VIRTUAL MONEY

The delinking of money with gold effectively turned the American dollar, and the other major currencies, into fiat money, and formalized money's switch from its real to its virtual phase. As always with money, though, the change was not widely advertised. There is a reason modern central bank buildings are designed to resemble ancient Roman temples. Unlike John Law, Nixon had made sure that the bankers were onside first. And as Galbraith noted, "Men did not speak of the final abandonment of the gold standard. Instead it was said that the gold window had been closed. No one could get much excited about the closing of a window." In fact, the only difference was that there was no formal connection to any reserve of gold, in Fort Knox, or the Fed or anywhere.

The virtual side of money was also evident in the plethora of new financial innovations that occurred in the post-war era, from the first credit cards in the 1950s, to automated teller machines in the 1960s, to electronic stock markets and option exchanges in the 1970s and 1980s, to internet banking in the 1990s, to cybercurrencies from the 2000s.

The role of the private financial sector has also increased dramatically. In fact, the vast majority of money in developed countries (about 97 per cent in the UK, for example) is produced not by central banks, but through loans by private banks, often in the form of mortgages. The Hartlibian idea of a land bank has been realized in the

"WE WILL PRESS FOR THE NECESSARY REFORMS TO SET UP AN URGENTLY NEEDED NEW INTERNATIONAL MONETARY SYSTEM."

RICHARD NIXON

form of instruments such as homeowner lines of credit, which allow people to use their houses as cash machines. Former chairman of the UK's Financial Services Authority Adair Turner noted that the amount of private credit and money that banks can create is "potentially infinite", just as the alchemists predicted. And yet: "To a quite striking extent, the role of banks in creating credit, money and purchasing power, was written out of the script of modern macro-economics."

Perhaps the biggest experiment with virtual money, though, was the establishment of the euro, which, unlike the dollar, was designed from the outset as a fiat currency.

The idea for a common European currency was first proposed at the League of Nations in 1929, and finally came to fruition on 1 January, 1999, when – after satisfying a range of convergence criteria for things like

• Opposite: The euro was introduced in 1999 by 11 European countries and is now used by 19.

inflation, interest rates, and government borrowing – 11 European countries officially adopted the euro as a unit of account. The first actual coins and notes were issued in 2002, replacing the legacy currencies which were removed from circulation. The euro is now used, at last count, by 19 of the European Union's 27 member states, with most of the remainder intending to adopt it in the future.

One of the architects of the euro was the Columbia University economist Robert Mundell, who was awarded the Nobel Memorial Prize in Economic Sciences in 1999 for his work on the idea of an "optimal currency area." It wasn't obvious that the European Union met all the required conditions, such as high labour mobility; however for a continent scarred by war, monetary unification promised much more than just eliminating the need for currency exchange, or the hope that shared monetary constraints would impose fiscal discipline on politicians: it promised a new European identity.

The European Union was described by political scientist John Ruggie in 1993 as the world's "first truly postmodern international political form" because of the way in which it plays around with classical concepts such as sovereignty and territoriality, and the designers of euro notes took a similarly postmodern approach, decorating the bills not with human figures, but with representations of windows, doors, and archways in a mix of historical styles, and structures such as bridges and viaducts.

One complication of the euro is that the European Central Bank has no fiscal branch or powerful central government to back it up. Instead, these functions are handled at a national level. As economists including L. Randall Wray warned in 1988, this effectively means that member countries "operate fiscal policy in a foreign currency; deficit spending will require borrowing in that foreign currency."

The idea that a virtual currency can act as a unifying bond has been sorely tested by events such as the 2007–8 financial crisis, where Greece was nearly ejected from the eurozone; and while the euro has taken its place as the second most-traded world currency after the dollar, it remains under stress today. Its continued but conflicted status as a transnational virtual currency is testament to the fact that we live in an era when money is both exceedingly important to our lives, but at the same time more abstract, obscure, and effervescent than ever. In the next chapter, we look at how economists have tried to make sense of the confounding properties of money – by basically ignoring them.

5

MONEY AND ECONOMICS

IF YOU ASK A NON-ECONOMIST WHAT ECONOMICS IS ABOUT, THEY MIGHT GUESS THAT IT HAS SOMETHING TO DO WITH MONEY. INDEED, IF MONEY TALKS, THEN SURELY ECONOMISTS ARE THE INTERPRETERS WHO TRANSLATE ITS STRANGE UTTERANCES INTO NORMAL LANGUAGE. HOWEVER THE REALITY IS SOMEWHAT DIFFERENT, STARTING WITH HOW THE SUBJECT IS DEFINED.

The most common definition of economics, which dates to the English economist Lionel Robbins in 1932, is that "Economics is a science which studies human behaviour as a relationship between ends and scarce means which have alternative uses." Or as it is often paraphrased, economics is the science of scarcity. So there is no mention of money at all.

When money is discussed, as mentioned in Chapter 1 it has traditionally been described as an inert medium of exchange, of little interest as a thing in itself. The economist Paul Samuelson described money in his bestselling textbook *Economics* as "*anything that serves as a commonly accepted medium of exchange*" (his emphasis). However, while this seems an adequate description of how money is *used*, it doesn't seem to get at the essence of what money *is* – or why it has such a hold over the human psyche.

In recent years, and especially following the financial crisis of 2007–08, this disinterested approach towards money has changed somewhat as behavioural economists and others have explored the role of psychology in financial transactions, probing phenomena such as financial bubbles. But even there, money is often treated as an objective measure of utility. Which leads to the question, what does money mean in economics – and why is it so often ignored or downplayed?

Of course, one response might be that if money doesn't matter much to economics, then maybe economics doesn't matter to money either, so it isn't an important topic for a

• Right: Lionel Robbins offered perhaps the most famous definition of economics.

• Opposite: Paul Samuelson, one of the 20th century's most celebrated economists and monetary theorists.

book on money. Yet (and perhaps despite its intentions) economics has still largely shaped our ideas about money and, therefore, money itself – so a history of money is in part a history of economics. In this chapter, we will unpick the complicated relationship between money and economics, beginning with the person who is widely considered to be the founder of modern economics, and the inventor of the "invisible hand" catch-phrase, Adam Smith.

THE INVISIBLE HAND

While Smith is best known today for his 1776 book *The Wealth of Nations*, which is widely regarded as a major attempt at turning economics into an objective science, some insight into his motivations is provided by his lesser-known *History of Astronomy*, which was written around 1758 but not published until after his death. Here Smith examines "all the different systems of nature" and shows how the scientific method, as epitomized by the "superior genius and sagacity of Sir Isaac Newton", managed to reduce the world's "chaos of jarring and discordant appearances" to a simple set of physical laws so that "all the appearances, which he joins together by it, necessarily follow." Smith's aim was to do something similar for the economy, though without all the equations.

> ## "IT IS NOT FROM THE BENEVOLENCE OF THE BUTCHER, THE BREWER, OR THE BAKER THAT WE EXPECT OUR DINNER, BUT FROM THEIR REGARD TO THEIR OWN INTEREST."
>
> **ADAM SMITH,** *THE WEALTH OF NATIONS*

In the same book, Smith makes his first mention of the invisible hand, in a passage about the tendency for polytheistic religions to interpret events as being caused by gods: "the invisible hand of Jupiter". In *The Theory of Moral Sentiments* (1759), he wrote that the rich are "led by an invisible hand" to "divide with the poor the produce of all their improvements … and thus without intending it, without knowing it, advance the interest of the society". Today, this might be called trickle-down economics. Finally, in *Wealth of Nations*, the phrase pops up again in a section on trade policy,

in which an individual is again "led by an invisible hand to promote an end which was no part of his intention".

Smith didn't use the phrase again in his own writings but the idea that people acting out of self-interest can lead to optimal outcomes was for him the economic equivalent of a Newtonian law of gravity, promising to calm the chaos of economic appearances. A first step in this project was to calm the chaos of money or, actually, make it go away.

In *Wealth of Nations*, Smith began by asserting that money was just a commodity, whose value is determined by the weight of precious metal contained. "By the money-price of goods, it is to be observed, I understand always the quantity of pure gold or silver for which they are sold, without any regard to the denomination of the coin."

While this answered the question of how money gets its value, what about things that aren't made of metal? Smith found the answer in a labour theory of value. Just as the value of money could be reduced to a mass of metal, so the value of a product could be measured as an expenditure of human energy. As he wrote, "The real price of every thing, what every thing really costs to the man who wants to acquire it, is the toil and trouble of acquiring it." The theory was illustrated using simple conceptual examples: "If among a nation of hunters, for example, it usually costs twice the labour to kill a beaver which it does to kill a deer, one beaver should naturally exchange for or be worth two deer."

In this quasi-Newtonian scheme, the price of an item – as measured by a mass of gold – was therefore determined by a quantity of energy, in the form of work, which put the economy on a reassuringly solid basis. The only factor complicating this equation was that prices had a tendency not to stay still. For example, the cost of an ounce of gold might measure the labour needed to extract it, but it was also affected by the "fertility or barrenness" of mines. It was therefore necessary to strip out these effects by distinguishing between "real" and "nominal" prices. What counted was only relative prices. Today, economists do something similar through measures such as real GDP which measure economic growth after inflation is taken into account.

Smith interpreted the economy, not in terms of money or static wealth, but in terms of dynamic processes like production, exchange, and labour. He argued that a main

• Opposite: Adam Smith, almost universally regarded as the father of modern economics.

driver of economic growth was the division of labour into specialized tasks, which he saw as a natural human tendency: "This division of labour, from which so many advantages are derived, is not originally the effect of any human wisdom … It is the necessary, though very slow and gradual, consequence of a certain propensity in human nature which has in view no such extensive utility; the propensity to truck, barter, and exchange one thing for another."

The net result of this specialization and trade was that the economy takes care of our needs, even if each individual is only concerned about their own needs. "It is not from the benevolence of the butcher, the brewer, or the baker that we expect our dinner, but from their regard to their own interest. We address ourselves, not to their humanity but to their self-love." Or as Samuelson paraphrased in 1948: "Every individual, in pursuing only his own selfish good, was led, as if by an invisible hand, to achieve the best good for all, so that any interference with free competition by government was almost certain to be injurious." Thus was born the modern understanding of the invisible hand theory, with free markets now playing the part of Jupiter, the god of sky and thunder.

THE INDUSTRIAL REVOLUTION

Since the time of Smith, the field of economics has tried to present itself as something approximating an objective science, but the reality is that economic theories are always influenced by the historical context in which they are developed. Smith himself was writing at the time of the Industrial Revolution, which was an unprecedented period of economic growth. Prior to the mid-18th century, human economic output had remained fairly stable. That changed during Smith's day with the emergence of new manufacturing processes in Europe and the United States. Hand production shifted to steam-powered machines and then to mechanized factories. Industries affected included textiles, chemicals, iron production, transportation, and so on. Mechanization led to large increases in income and standards of living, as well as an increased rate of population growth.

Under the gold standard, money was defined in terms of gold. But unlike the mercantilist economists who had confused value with bullion, Smith identified wealth as the fruit of the markets that he saw growing and diversifying around him. His theory that value could be measured by gold,

produced by labour, and expanded through specialization and the spread of markets, made sense in this context. One corollary of this approach, which had lasting consequences, was that money dropped out of the analysis. The economist Jean-Baptiste Say, who popularized Smith's work in France,

"IF YOU GO BACK TO 1800, EVERYBODY WAS POOR. I MEAN EVERYBODY. THE INDUSTRIAL REVOLUTION KICKED IN, AND A LOT OF COUNTRIES BENEFITED."
BILL GATES

summed this up in his statement that "money is a veil", although, as we'll see, it might be more accurate to say that it is the equations of economics that are the veil.

Smith's work was key not only to the foundation of economics, but also to the foundation of the United States. His *Wealth of Nations* was published in 1776, the year of the American Revolution, and his book had a profound and long-lasting influence on the country. The US economist George Akerlof describes the "central ideology" of the United States as conforming to "the fundamental view of Adam Smith" which even today "drives huge amounts of policy".

The next revolution in economics was also a product of historical context – but this time it was driven by the growth, not of industry, but of finance. And its influence would prove equally enduring.

THE RAILWAY MANIA

The Industrial Revolution was driven by a growth in manufacturing, specialization, transportation, and international trade, which all involved the production and exchange of real things, such as goods and labour. Of course, building things like factories and railways required a great deal of money, but classical economists (as we now call them) such as Smith saw capital in terms of things rather than the money itself. Savings and profits were assumed to be directly channeled into physical purchases. What counted was the real thing, not the virtual number.

• Opposite: A sketch for James Watt's revolutionary steam engine.

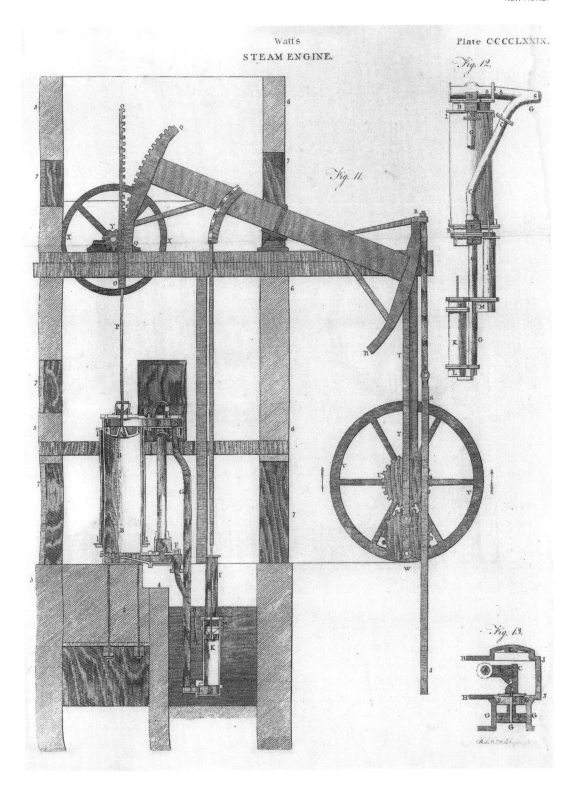

Watt's
STEAM ENGINE.

Plate CCCCLXXIX.

Fig. 12.

Fig. 11.

Fig. 13.

By the mid-19th century, the virtual side of the economy was beginning to assert itself with the proliferation of financial markets for things like stocks and bonds. An example was the Railway Mania that took place in the UK and Ireland in the 1840s. As industry expanded, things needed to be moved, but canals or horse-drawn carts couldn't handle the traffic.

The world's first, proper inter-city railway was the Liverpool and Manchester Railway (L&MR), which opened in 1830. Similar railways expanded across the country, raising money by selling stocks on the stock market. Investor excitement grew as share prices climbed, which attracted more investors, and more stock-market listings. At the mania's peak in 1846 some 272 Acts of Parliament were passed for the purpose of incorporating new railroad companies, which together proposed a total of 9,500 miles of track.

Of course, the bubble soon burst, and share prices fell by over 50 per cent in the course of a few years. Many of the companies collapsed, or turned out to be fraudulent enterprises in the first place. In many respects, the Railway Mania was the 19th-century version of the dot-com boom, where a new technology is initially over-hyped, but has positive long-term consequences.

In this case, the speculative boom gave the UK not just an excellent rail system, but also helped create the modern stock market. The idea of making financial investments was legitimized and popularized through the spread of information sources such as brochures, manuals, and articles in local and national newspapers which were, for the first time, becoming widely affordable. It suddenly became possible for the general public to think about investing in abstract markets, and to take a punt on a company at a price which was just a number on a stock list.

• Opposite: The surge in railway construction was not universally welcomed.

• Above: The opening of the Liverpool to Manchester railway in 1830.

"I FIND THAT THE NUMBER OF ACTS OF PARLIAMENT ... ARE THE BEST INDICATIONS OF AN APPROACHING PANIC."

WILLIAM STANLEY JEVONS

WILLIAM STANLEY JEVONS

One person to have been personally affected by the Railway Mania was the English economist William Stanley Jevons. His father was a Liverpool iron merchant and engineer who constructed one of the first iron boats, although the family firm went bankrupt following the 1847 crisis. Jevons attended University College London for two years, but because of financial pressure following the bankruptcy (student loans weren't yet a thing) he left to take a position as assayer at the new mint in Sydney, Australia. He spent five years there, before returning to the UK to resume his studies in logic and political economics.

The experience of the Railway Mania appears to have shaped his approach to economics, and he was one of the first economists to study the business cycle in detail. In the early 1860s he embarked on a project to build a "Statistical Atlas" consisting of diagrams on a number of economic topics, including the prediction of "commercial storms". As he told his brother Herbert in an 1861 letter, "I find that the number of Acts of Parliament, the number of patents, and the number of bricks manufactured, are the best indications of an approaching panic, which arises generally from a large investment of labour in works not immediately profitable, as machinery, canals, railways, etc."

• Above: Economist William Stanley Jevons established the theory of marginal utility.

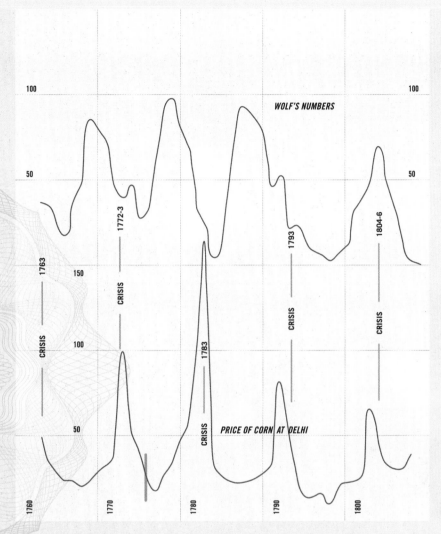

•Jevons's diagram showing fluctuations in sunspot activity (top line) and commercial activity as represented by the prices of corn at Delhi (bottom line).

Jevons' interest in the business cycle wasn't purely theoretical, since he also relied on investments himself. In another 1864 letter, he told Herbert that "railway dividends also are improved up to 6 per cent, so that I shall have an income of about £170, which fully covers expenses."

His own theory was that the business cycle was a periodic phenomenon driven, not by investor sentiment, but by sunspots. As he wrote in 1875: "If the planets govern the sun, and the sun governs the vintages and harvests, and thus the prices of food and raw materials and the state of the money market, it follows that the configurations of the planets may prove to be the remote causes of the greatest commercial disasters." The fact that the average business cycle, which he put at 10.5 years, did not perfectly match the sunspot cycle drew him into a long argument with astronomers over the quality of their observations.

In a world where you could live off your investments, which were listings in an exchange, whose prices were at the mercy of events happening some 93 million miles away on the surface of the sun, it is easy to imagine that a labour theory of value may not have appeared fit for purpose – which is what led Jevons to the theory of marginal utility.

• Left: Jeremy Bentham established the philosophical school of utilitarianism. His preserved body is on display at University College London.

MARGINAL UTILITY

In the second paragraph of his 1871 book *The Theory of Political Economy*, Jevons announced that, "Repeated reflection and inquiry have led me to the somewhat novel opinion that value depends entirely upon utility." The concept of utility – meaning roughly what is good or useful or pleasurable – was first proposed in the late 18th century by Jeremy Bentham, the English philosopher and social reformer, who defined it as that which appears to "augment or diminish the happiness of the party whose interest is in question".

Bentham was thinking about ways to maximize (he invented the word) the happiness of society as a whole, but the same idea could apply to the financial markets. For example, if you held investments in a railway company and they went up in price, then so did your utility.

More precisely, according to Jevons, exchange prices were determined by marginal utility, which takes into account whether you already have what is being offered. If you are thirsty, you will pay more for the first cup of water than for the seventh; if you are already rich, then a minor uptick in your stock portfolio will not cause you delight, even if the actual sum is substantial.

As Jevons wrote, the aim was to "treat Economy as a Calculus of Pleasure and Pain". Of course, utility is a psychological quantity that doesn't lend itself to direct measurement. He argued, however, that if utility is equated with value, then it can be measured through price: "I hesitate to say that men will ever have the means of measuring directly the feelings of the human heart. A unit of pleasure or of pain is difficult even to conceive; but it is the amount of these feelings which is continually prompting us to buying and selling, borrowing and lending, labouring and resting, producing and consuming; and it is from the quantitative effects of the feelings that we must estimate their comparative amounts. We can no more know nor measure gravity in its own nature than we can measure a feeling; but, just as we measure gravity by its effects in the motion of a pendulum, so we may estimate the equality or inequality of feelings by the decisions of the human mind. The will is our pendulum, and its oscillations are minutely registered in the price lists of the markets."

The economy could, therefore, be modelled using what Jevons called "a mechanics of utility and self-interest". The theory was similar to that of Adam Smith, with the difference that the quantity revealed by the market was utility rather than labour – and it would be measured in terms of price.

"THE GREATEST HAPPINESS OF THE GREATEST NUMBER IS THE FOUNDATION OF MORALS AND LEGISLATION."

JEREMY BENTHAM

NEOCLASSICAL ECONOMICS

The idea of marginal utility was clearly in the air, because it was arrived at independently around the same time by two other economists: Léon Walras in France, and Carl Menger in Austria. Like Jevons, they argued that the values of goods are determined by the utility they grant the consumer; that this utility diminished as the quantity of the good increases; and that markets act as a price discovery mechanism.

Unlike classical economists, who analysed the economy in terms of factors of production such as land, labour, and capital, these neoclassical economists, as they became known, put the focus on price. As Menger wrote in 1871, the aim was to establish "a price theory based upon reality". All three were also influenced by experience with finance and stock markets. Walras worked for a spell as a bank manager and based his model of a market economy on the Paris Bourse; Menger first became interested in economics in his mid-twenties while working as a newspaper reporter at the Vienna stock exchange.

In one sense, then, neoclassical economics seemed to be all about money; but really it was about price, which is not the same thing. After all, you can't pay someone with a price. As in classical economics, money was treated as a metric, or an inert medium of exchange, rather than as a thing in itself. For example, John Stuart Mill's 1848 book *Principles of Political Economy*, which served as a standard text for over 60 years, included chapters on the mechanics of money, but warned: "There cannot, in short, be intrinsically a more insignificant thing, in the economy of society, than money."

• Above: Neoclassical economists Carl Menger (left) and Léon Walras (right).

• Opposite: Irving Fisher (right) warned of the dangers of inflation.

• Overleaf: A Wall Street speculator tries to sell his car after losing all of his money in the stock market crash.

The main motivation for concentrating on price was because, as a numerical quantity, it lent itself to treatment using mathematical equations and physics-like laws. As Jevons put it, these laws were to be considered "as sure and demonstrative as that of kinematics or statics, nay, almost as self-evident as are the elements of Euclid, when the real meaning of the formulae is fully seized". Walras likewise described economics as "a science that resembles the physio-mathematical sciences in every respect".

In order to achieve this feat of mathematicizing the economy, economists had to make numerous simplifying assumptions. Jevons assumed that, "Every individual must be considered as exchanging from a pure regard to his own requirements or private interests, and there must be perfectly free competition." Variations in behaviour were assumed to average themselves out over a population, so what counted was the opinion of the "average man". Markets tended towards a self-regulated and stable equilibrium which balanced supply and demand. Walras attempted to demonstrate this using a mathematical model of an idealized economy. And, most importantly, money was a commodity like any other, playing no active role.

VELOCITY OF M2 MONEY STOCK

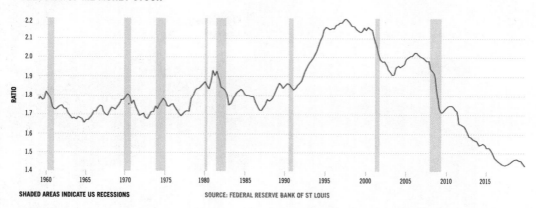

SOURCE: FEDERAL RESERVE BANK OF ST LOUIS

GROSS DOMESTIC PRODUCT

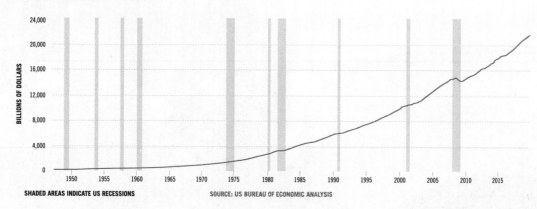

SOURCE: US BUREAU OF ECONOMIC ANALYSIS

• Above: Top panel shows a plot of the velocity of money in the US. Bottom panel shows a plot of Gross Domestic Product (GDP) in the US. Grey bands show recessions.

• Right: A 20 million mark note from the Weimar Republic is a vivid illustration of hyperinflation.

THE MONEY ILLUSION

The physics-like approach to economics was taken to the next level by the American economist Irving Fisher. In 1891 he received Yale University's first PhD in economics. In his thesis, which was published in book form as *Mathematical Investigations in the Theory of Value and Prices*, he made an explicit link between concepts in mechanics and economics, with particle mapping to individual, space to commodity, force to marginal utility, and energy to utility.

The role of money in this picture was relegated to the control of inflation, which Fisher explained through the equation MV = PT. Here M is the amount of money in circulation, V is the average rate (called the velocity) at which the money changes hands, P is the average transaction price, and T is the total volume of transactions. The left-hand side MV represents the flow of money through the economy – if a pound coin changes hands three times in a year, then it represents £3 in total transactions. The right-hand side PT, aggregated over a country, amounts to what today is called the Gross Domestic Product (GDP).

The equation therefore says that GDP equals money times velocity, which is just an accounting identity, since economic activity is measured by the flow of money. If money is hoarded, so that the average velocity decreases, then this slows the economy. Fisher applied the equation by assuming that the velocity V and the number of transactions T are fixed. If this is the case, then boosting the money supply M by 4 per cent will just increase the price level P by the same amount. It follows that the central bank can control inflation by watching the money supply – if inflation is climbing, just tap on the monetary brakes.

From a theoretical point of view, inflation shouldn't really matter, because as Smith and the other classical economists had taught, what counts is real prices after inflation is stripped out. But Fisher argued that inflation was harmful because of what he called the "money illusion" which was our tendency to think in terms of nominal prices. It is hard to compare prices across time periods when inflation is significant – selling your house for double its purchase price sounds less impressive if the cost of living has also doubled. Inflation also means that businesses have to keep raising prices, which is hard to do without losing customers.

Fisher's equation later formed the basis of the theory known as monetarism. Its best-known exponent was the American economist Milton Friedman, who said in 1970 that, "Inflation is always and everywhere a monetary phenomenon in the sense that it is and can be produced only by a more rapid increase in the quantity of money than in output." As discussed later, inflation has proved to be rather more complicated than that.

MONEY IGNORED

To summarize, both classical and neoclassical economics were shaped by their historical contexts. Classical economics was a reaction to the dynamism of the Industrial Revolution, and focused on things like land, labour, and capital, where the latter referred to things like factories and infrastructure rather than money. It improved on mercantilism by showing that economic growth was about much more than just accumulating treasure, and it laid the foundations for the development of economics as a kind of social mechanics. In the process, it effectively removed money from the calculations.

Neoclassical economics turned the labour theory of value on its head, by arguing that prices of everything, including labour, reflect the subjective quality of utility. By reducing the complex idea of value to a number, it allowed economists to mathematicize the economy, and treat it as the equivalent of a physical system. Again money was excluded from the analysis, except for technical issues such as the control of inflation.

As economics progressed in the 20th century, it continued to be affected by events in the real economy. In Europe, the school of economics known as "ordoliberalism", which emphasises price stability, was shaped by the hyperinflation which occurred in countries such as Austrian and Germany after the First World War. In the 1930s, the Great Depression led to the development of Keynesian economics – named for the English economist John Maynard Keynes – which advocated using government money to stimulate the economy during times of recession.

The so-called "Great Moderation" in the last two decades of the 20th century, marked by a reduction in the volatility of the business cycle, was accompanied by a return to the cozy certitudes of neoclassical economics – until the Global Financial Crisis of 2007–08 sent economists back once again to the drawing boards. The crisis had a particularly heavy impact on the eurozone, whose design flaws were exposed when a number of member countries (Greece, Portugal, Ireland, Spain and Cyprus) found themselves in urgent need of a bailout in order to pay their debts, leading to much tension with ordoliberalists.

Ironically, while mainstream economics teaches that asset prices are drawn by what Alan Greenspan once called the "global invisible hand" to a natural equilibrium, one of the world's more stable currencies is the Chinese renminbi, which is governed by the very visible hand of the Chinese state. Unlike most other central banks, the People's Bank of China is not independent from the governing party, in this case the Communist Party of China. Until 2005, the value of the renminbi, whose basic unit is the yuan, was pegged to the US dollar, however the exchange rate has since been allowed to float within a narrow band. International use of the currency has increased with the growing clout of the Chinese economy, and in 2015 the International Monetary Fund decided to add it to its "special drawing rights" basket of reserve currencies, where it joined the dollar, euro, pound, and yen. China's expanding influence has also highlighted questions in economics around the role of institutions and the causes of economic development.

To summarize, money might not play a big role in economics, but financial events including booms and busts have certainly shaped the development of the field.

At the same time, the field of economics has long downplayed the importance of money. The effect of this, ironically, has been to make money more important, and its effects more volatile and potentially dangerous, than ever – exactly because we don't have a theoretical framework with which to understand and address some of its wilder tendencies.

In the next chapter, we look in more detail at the phenomenon of economic crises, and show how a theory of value led to one of the largest destructions of value ever seen.

"I NOW SEE NOTHING TO GIVE GROUND TO HOPE – NOTHING OF MAN."

FORMER PRESIDENT CALVIN COOLIDGE ON THE GREAT DEPRESSION, 1932

• Opposite: *Migrant Mother*, 1936, by photographer Dorothea Lange. The archetypal image of the suffering experienced during the Great Depression.

6

BOOM AND BUST

AS SEEN IN THE PREVIOUS CHAPTER, ECONOMISTS HAVE LONG EMPHASIZED THE
NOTION THAT MARKETS DRIVE PRICES TO AN EQUILIBRIUM VALUE WHICH REFLECTS
INTRINSIC VALUE, AND HAVE SOUGHT STABLE LAWS WHICH CUT THROUGH WHAT
ADAM SMITH CALLED THE "CHAOS OF JARRING AND DISCORDANT APPEARANCES"
THAT IS THE LIVING WORLD. AND YET ONE OF THE MOST PERSISTENT FEATURES
OF THE ECONOMY IS THAT IT SEEMS HIGHLY UNSTABLE, AS SHOWN BY THE
PHENOMENON OF FINANCIAL BOOMS AND BUSTS.

A number of economists have theorized that booms and
busts are signs of a deeper, cyclical order. William Stanley
Jevons, for example, observed in 1878 that "considerable
crises occurred in England in the years 1763, 1772, 1782
or 1783, and 1793, and I have discovered some indications
of a crisis in 1753", which seemed to fit his sunspot theory.

Other economists over the years have argued that the
economy has regular cycles, whose timescales correspond
to fluctuations in some aspect of the economy. Jevons's
contemporary, the French economist Clément Juglar,
independently found a boom/bust cycle in investment of
9 to 11 years, and identified four phases: prosperity, crisis,
liquidation, and recession. Other such cycles identified by
economists include the Kuznets infrastructure cycle of 15 to
25 years; the Kondratiev technology wave of 45 to 60 years;
and a shorter Kitchin cycle for inventory of 40 months.

In his 1939 book *Business Cycles*, the economist Joseph
Schumpeter proposed that economic fluctuations were
caused by all these different cycles adding together, as he
believed occurred at the start of the Great Depression. But
do these booms and busts really follow regular patterns, or
is it more accurate to say that they are driven by the unseen
chaos of money? In one report, the International Monetary
Fund analysed "151 systemic banking crises episodes around
the globe during 1970–2017" which – at an average of over
three a year – suggests a certain lack of reliability on the part
of the financial system. In this chapter, we show how the

• Above: Joseph Schumpeter popularized the
concept of creative destruction.

intrinsically unstable nature of money manifests itself in the
larger economy – and how economic theories which ignore
this instability are themselves a factor driving financial crises.

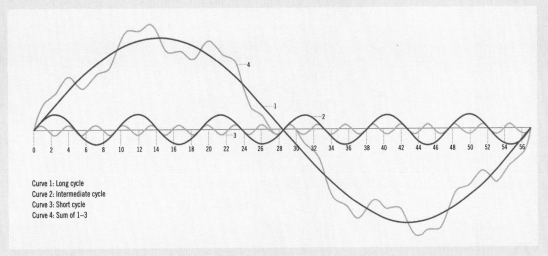

Curve 1: Long cycle
Curve 2: Intermediate cycle
Curve 3: Short cycle
Curve 4: Sum of 1–3

• Schumpeter's model of the business cycle, which superposed regular cycles of different frequencies to simulate economic fluctuations.

THE MADNESS OF PEOPLE

In his 1841 book *Extraordinary Popular Delusions and the Madness of Crowds*, the Scottish journalist Charles Mackay documented a number of economic booms and busts throughout history. An early example was the Dutch "tulip mania" of 1637 which apparently saw the price of the newly introduced tulip bulb soar to a point where a single bulb cost ten times the annual wage of a skilled artisan. According to Mackay, everyone was in on the action: "Nobles, citizens, farmers, mechanics, seamen, footmen, maidservants, even chimney sweeps and old clotheswomen, dabbled in tulips." At least until, rather suddenly, the bloom came off their investments.

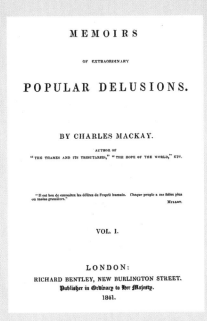

• Far Left: Charles Mackay's book is a classic account of human folly.

• Left, bottom: A Dutch tulip.

• Overleaf: Brueghel the Younger satirized the "tulip mania" of the 17th century.

Mackay's book listed a number of other such "popular delusions" including John Law's Mississippi Company, and a later edition included the Railway Mania of the 1840s. Perhaps the case study which resonates most today, however, was the South Sea Company episode of the early 18th century, which first put the word "bubble" into the financial vocabulary.

The South Sea Company was established as a public–private partnership in 1711 that was supposed to help fund the English national debt. In return, it was granted a permanent monopoly on trade with Mexico and South America. In particular, the company was given the right to carry African slaves to Spanish ports in the New World. The only catch was

that the area was controlled by Spain, with whom England was at war – but the company directors assured the public that this would be taken care of during peace negotiations.

The company's public relations efforts were assisted by writers such as Daniel Defoe and Jonathan Swift, who were paid to write articles promoting the scheme. Part of their job was to give the public a positive view of the brutal Atlantic slave trade. This was done by emphasizing the exotic nature of the locations, and what one anonymous author (possibly Defoe) called the "inexhaustible Fountain" of gold and silver available in the New World. These wordsmiths later applied their literary skills to novels including Defoe's *Robinson Crusoe*, and Swift's *Gulliver's Travels*.

Having raised money, the company managed to arrange some slave-trade voyages, but these turned out to be more complicated and expensive than anticipated, and it isn't clear whether they were ever profitable. In any case, the directors preferred to concentrate on the safer business of financial engineering. Inspired by John Law's Mississippi venture (which had yet to implode), the company made a bid to triple its share of the national debt to almost the full amount,

• Opposite: The "Wagon of Fools", one of many satirical images aimed at "tulip mania".

• Above: Another example of folly and popular delusion, the South Sea Company scandal of 1720.

at better terms than their rival the Bank of England. Eased along by bribes in the form of stock offerings to politicians and influential people like King George's mistresses, the

• Daniel Defoe (above) and Jonathan Swift (opposite) helped popularize the notion of a financial bubble.

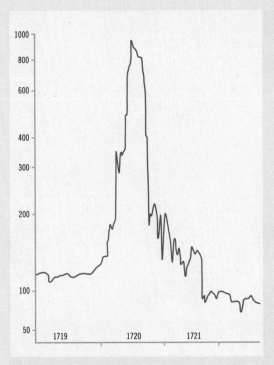

• Chart of the South Sea Company stock price.

• Opposite: Scottish poet and songwriter Charles MacKay was a critic of the stock market bubbles.

• Opposite (inset): Cover of the English translation of the Asiento contract signed by Britain and Spain in 1713 as part of the Utrecht treaty that ended the War of Spanish Succession. The contract granted exclusive rights to Britain to sell slaves in the Spanish Indies.

"I CAN CALCULATE THE MOTIONS OF HEAVENLY BODIES, BUT NOT THE MADNESS OF PEOPLE."

ISAAC NEWTON

man quickly sold a thousand shares – at which point he fled to Europe.

As Mackay commented, "The public mind was in a state of unwholesome fermentation. Men were no longer satisfied with the slow but sure profits of cautious industry." Meanwhile the directors at the South Sea Company, sensing perhaps that optimism had peaked, began to sell their shares.

This did not go unnoticed – or perhaps the mania had just run its course. The stock price stabilized, then wobbled, then started to sink, and by the end of September the price had collapsed back to £135. As Jonathan Swift (no longer on the payroll) wrote:

Subscribers here by thousands float
And jostle one another down
Each paddling in his leaky boat
And here they fish for gold, and drown.

The company directors were villified as "crocodiles and cannibals". The company treasurer, Mr Knight, put on a disguise, boarded a specially chartered boat – and left for Europe.

The crisis caused a record number of bankruptcies at every level of society. Isaac Newton himself lost a large part of his fortune, which led him to conclude that, "I can calculate the motions of heavenly bodies, but not the madness of people." In response, the government passed the Bubble Act in 1721. (The use of the term "bubble" in this context was probably first due to Defoe, though Swift helped popularize it.) This forbade the founding of joint-stock companies without a royal charter – but it didn't manage to ban bubbles, which have remained a feature of the world economy.

If Mackay were alive today, he would have updated his book with the dot-com bubble that burst in 2000, the US housing bubble of 2006, and any number of other such events. Economists would try to ban bubbles in another way – by saying that they didn't exist.

company's proposal was accepted – which was when the mania started to grow. As rumours of increasing trade spread through the coffee houses in the City of London, the stock rose in the first half of 1720 by more than a factor of five, to about £1,000.

As always, the excitement in the stock market stimulated the energies of entrepreneurs, as people tried to cash in on the buzz by proposing their own schemes. Company prospectuses in the same year included some trying to develop methods for "perpetual motion", "extracting silver from lead", and "the transmutation of quicksilver into a malleable fine metal". One man even announced a company for "carrying on an undertaking of great advantage, but nobody to know what it is". Five thousand shares of £100 would be issued, with a deposit of £2 per share, and a promised pay-off of £100 pounds per year, per share. The

THE ASSIENTO;

OR

CONTRACT

FOR

Allowing to the Subjects of *Great Britain* the Liberty of Importing NEGROES into the *Spanish America.*

Sign'd by the CATHOLICK KING at *Madrid*, the Twenty fixth Day of *March*, 1713.

By Her Majesties Special Command.

· LONDON,
Printed by *John Baskett*, Printer to the Queens most Excellent Majesty And by the Assigns of *Thomas Newcomb*, and *Henry Hills*, deceas'd. 1713.

THE INVISIBLE HAND THEOREM

In the years following the end of the Second World War, when the United States and Russia were locked in the icy embrace of the Cold War, American economists focused on developing a consistent economic theory that combined neoclassical economics with some of the aspects of Keynesianism. This "neoclassical synthesis", as Paul Samuelson called it, was based on the related principles of maximization and equilibrium. Firms and individuals act rationally to maximize utility, and this drives markets – and the economy as a whole – towards a stable equilibrium. Issues such as imperfect competition were treated as "frictions" which policy makers could aim to minimize.

In the 1950s, the economists Kenneth Arrow and Gérard Debreu developed a model of an idealized market economy and used it to prove that the market, if left to its own devices, would attain an optimal equilibrium, in which nothing can be changed without making at least one person worse off, a condition known as Pareto optimality. The result became known as the "invisible hand theorem" because it seemed to provide mathematical proof of Smith's theory that free markets are inherently self-stabilizing and set prices to their optimal levels.

The Arrow–Debreu model has long been considered the crown jewel of neoclassical economics, and inspired the development of the equilibrium models which are still used by policy makers today. To achieve its mathematically elegant result, the model relied on extending the powers of rational economic man to include things like infinite

computational power and the ability to devise plans for every future eventuality. The model also represented what amounted to a barter economy so had no role for money. Finally, another slight glitch with the equilibrium approach was that, when economists tried to apply it to the real economy, they found that it was of little or no use for making relevant predictions. For example, it couldn't be used to predict the onset of a recession, or determine whether a bubble was about to implode, because these things weren't even a feature of the model.

Economics was becoming increasingly mathematical, which gave it the aura of a genuine science. But the main test of a scientific model has traditionally been its ability to make accurate predictions – and economic models failed the test. As the former Federal Reserve Chairman Paul Volcker later complained in a 2019 book, "There are hundreds of economists poring over their computers,

• Below: Kenneth Arrow (left) and Gérard Debreu (right) developed a model of the idealized market economy

but I think they have just demonstrated their inability to be forecasters."

One excuse for poor predictive performance was that the economy is vulnerable to external shocks, such as a hike in oil prices, that are inherently unpredictable, or which violate the model assumptions. Another reason was that the economy is so complex that no model can perfectly capture its fluctuations. An innovative excuse for forecast error was supplied by the American economist Eugene Fama, who argued that markets were unpredictable because they were so efficient. As we'll see, Fama's theorem would eventually form the basis for the latest version of the financial philosopher's stone that promised an apparently unlimited generation of money – but would also lead to one of the biggest bubbles and crashes in financial history.

EFFICIENT MARKETS

Fama's efficient market hypothesis, which was published in a 1965 PhD thesis, assumed that markets for things like stocks are made up of "large numbers of rational profit-maximizers" who have access to perfect information,

and that market forces drive the price of any security to its correct "intrinsic value". Price changes were driven by random news so were inherently unpredictable.

As with the Arrow–Debreu model, the theory reinforced Smith's argument that market price equals intrinsic value, and the idea that markets are inherently rational, efficient, and optimal. A corrollary was that in an efficient market, bubbles were effectively impossible. As Fama later said, "I don't even know what a bubble means."

Of course, for many people, the idea that group opinion is a reliable guide to the truth will seems counterintuitive. The philosopher John Locke wrote of it that "there cannot be a more dangerous thing to rely on, nor more likely to mislead, one; since there is so much more Falshood and Errour amongst Men, than Truth and Knowledge." Not to mention Mackay's "Madness of Crowds". But economists were willing to roll with it.

• Left: Eugene Fama, pioneer of the efficient markets hypothesis.

One reason was that, while the idea that market prices are unpredictable might seem like bad news, the theory held out the promise of a different kind of prediction. If one assumes that market fluctuations are truly random events, like the toss of dice or the spin of a roulette wheel, then it is possible to calculate risk based on statistical methods by looking at how prices have changed in the past. One may not be able to predict whether or not a stock will rise or fall in price by 10 per cent over the next year, but one can calculate the probability of it doing so. This allowed the development of techniques to calculate the risk of financial derivatives such as options, which in turn helped grow the market for those derivatives.

PRICING OPTIONS

One question that had long troubled economists was how to price the financial instruments known as options. These give the buyer the right – but not the obligation – to buy or sell a particular asset for a set price, known as the strike price, at some future date. They derive their value from the underlying asset, hence the term derivative. Options had been sold

at stock exchanges in places like London and Amsterdam since the 17th century, but they were generally viewed as a disreputable way of gambling on stock price movements. In the United States, they came close to being outlawed after the crash of 1929, and even in the 1960s were only available for trade in a small New York market. It also didn't help that there was no agreed method on how to cost them.

For example, if the price of a stock today is £100, then how much should you pay for an option which allows you to buy it in six months' time for £80? If the stock falls to less than £80, then the option is worthless. In fact, if the return on your investment in the option is less than what you could get from a risk-free investment such as a government bond, then you have effectively lost money because you could have put your money there instead. On the other hand, if the stock price goes to £120 after six months, then you can exercise the option, purchase the stock for £80, then turn around and sell it the same day at £120 for a nominal £40 profit.

Consequently, the price of the option depends on a host of factors. Some of these, such as the current price of the stock (here £100), the time to maturity (six months), and

the strike price (£80), are specified by the contract. But the big unknown is how to assess the probability that the stock will end up above or below the strike price. And this is where efficient market theory came in. If price changes are random, but follow a stable statistical distribution, then one can compute the probability of the price moving by a certain amount up or down over the duration of the option.

The French mathematician Louis Bachelier had come close to working out the formula for option pricing in his PhD thesis *Théorie de la spéculation*, published in 1900. The final formula, which took into account effects such as the risk-free interest rate, was only published in 1973 by the University of Chicago's Fischer Black and Myron Scholes, with some help from MIT's Robert C. Merton.

The existence of a mathematical formula changed the whole story around options. Instead of gambling, they were a clever form of risk management. The method, which was inspired by and dependent on efficient market theory, also came out at an auspicious time, given that the Chicago Board Options Exchange opened for business the same year. As its counsel explained: "Black–Scholes was really what enabled

• Opposite: The New York Stock Exchange.

• Top: "Derivatives" on a screen. The stock market is increasingly digitalised.

• Above: Fischer Black, a pioneer in working out hedging formulas.

the exchange to thrive ... it gave a lot of legitimacy to the whole notions of hedging and efficient pricing, whereas we were faced, in the late 60s–early 70s with the issue of gambling. That issue fell away, and I think Black–Scholes made it fall away. It wasn't speculation or gambling, it was efficient pricing." It also didn't hurt that in 1977 Texas Instruments came out with a special version of their hand-held calculator that could run the Black–Scholes formula.

Even better, the formula seemed to promise a perfect, automated system for making money. Anyone who understood the formula – or at least could run it on their calculator – could use it to exploit anomalies and mispricings in

• Left: Myron Scholes, one of the developers of the Black–Scholes trading formula.

• Above: The Chicago Board Options Exchange.

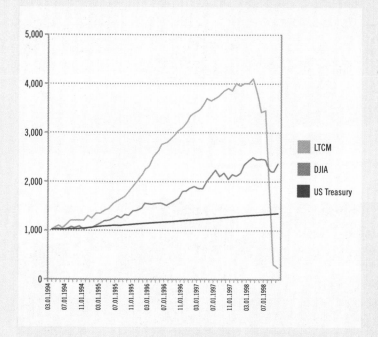

5,000

4,000

3,000

2,000

1,000

0

LTCM

DJIA

US Treasury

03.01.1994 07.01.1994 11.01.1994 03.01.1995 07.01.1995 11.01.1995 03.01.1996 07.01.1996 11.01.1996 03.01.1997 07.01.1997 11.01.1997 03.01.1998 07.01.1998

• The value of $1,000 invested from March 1994 to November 1998 in Long-Term Capital Management, the Dow Jones Industrial Average, or risk-free US Treasuries.

the markets. Of course, the formula relied on numerous assumptions, such as that markets are perfectly competitive and efficient. But the fact that there was an agreed formula meant that traders were all on the same page.

A quarter century after the formula was published, Scholes and Merton were awarded the 1997 Nobel Memorial Prize in Economics for their work on option pricing (Black had died). By this time, Scholes and Merton were partners in a hedge fund called Long-Term Capital Management, which used its expertise in option pricing to construct complicated and highly leveraged financial bets. According to Scholes, the business model boiled down to "vacuuming up nickels that others couldn't see". The strategy was highly profitable. When asked if he had more money or brains, Scholes replied,

"Brains, but it's getting close." It all fell apart in August 1998 when, in strict defiance of efficient market theory, the Russian government decided to default on its bonds. The company had to be rescued at a cost of $3.6 billion.

The debacle exposed a flaw in the model, which is that abstract theory doesn't work so well in a crisis, when no one wants to execute your orders. As one risk manager from Merrill Lynch complained, "We had no ideas they would have trouble – these people were known for risk management. They had taught it; they designed it … God knows, we were dealing with Nobel Prize winners!" This, however, was just a warm-up for a much larger crisis, which again had its roots in a mathematical model, and the complex and unpredictable dynamics of money.

"ONCE A TYPHOON BREAKS LOOSE IN MARKETS, THERE IS NO TELLING WHERE IT WILL GO."

ROGER LOWENSTEIN, *WHEN GENIUS FAILED: THE RISE AND FALL OF LONG-TERM CAPITAL MANAGEMENT*

HOW TO MAKE MONEY

According to Copernicus, an excess of money leads to inflation. And one way to increase the money supply, as the Hartlibians knew, is to increase credit. Every time a private bank makes a new loan, it creates new money which adds to the money supply.

Normally, we think of inflation in terms of the costs of everyday expenses such as food and clothing but inflation also occurs in financial assets such as stocks or real estate. If the financial system finds a way to generate new loans, and most of these loans end up being used to purchase financial assets, then a positive feedback loop is set up. Someone borrows money to buy an asset; the asset goes up in value because other people are making similar investments; the rise in value means that the financial position of both the borrower and the bank have improved, allowing more loans to be issued; and so on.

> ## "BECAUSE OF THE DISPERSION OF FINANCIAL RISKS TO THOSE MORE WILLING AND ABLE TO BEAR THEM, THE ECONOMY AND FINANCIAL SYSTEM ARE MORE RESILIENT."
>
> **BEN BERNANKE**

The key step in this loop is figuring out a way to generate new loans, which in turn relies on managing perceptions of risk. Banks are usually only willing to lend if they are sure of getting their money back, and as a minimum will demand some form of risk-free collateral. In John Law's Mississippi bubble, investments in the Mississippi Company were backed by the apparently risk-free money printed by the Banque Royale, as well as by the more ephemeral promise of unlimited American gold. In the early 2000s, this enabling role was performed by the invention of sophisticated financial instruments such as collateralized debt obligations (CDOs), which seemed to remove risk through the use of complicated mathematics.

A CDO is a clever way of taking the cash flows from many underlying assets, pooling them all together, and then paying them out in tranches. For example, if a CDO aggregates the payments from a thousand mortgages, then the senior tranche gets paid first, then the next tranche, all the way down to the junk tranche. The further down you are, the higher the risk that you won't get paid in case some of the mortgages default. Each tranche has its own credit rating, so the senior tranche might be AAA but will also be the most expensive. For banks, the main advantage of the CDO was that it allowed them to package up large numbers of loans and sell them off to investors. This removed the risk from their balance sheets, clearing the way to make more loans.

According to mainstream economics, which ignored the money creation aspect, this was all to the good. In 2000, Alan Greenspan, then Chairman of the Federal Reserve, testified to Congress that the ability to eliminate risk through such derivatives had made the financial system more robust: "I believe that the general growth in large institutions has occurred in the context of an underlying structure in markets in which many of the larger risks are dramatically – I should say fully – hedged." In 2006, the International Monetary Fund (IMF) noted that, "The dispersion of credit risk by banks to a broader and more diverse group of investors, rather than warehousing such risks on their balance sheets, has helped to make the banking and overall financial system more resilient." Greenspan's successor at the Federal Reserve, Ben Bernanke, agreed the same year that "because of the dispersion of financial risks to those more willing and able to bear them, the economy and financial system are more resilient."

The main effect of these financial instruments, however, was not to remove risk, but to unleash an expansion in credit, and create massive amounts of asset price inflation, particularly in US real estate. As with all financial bubbles, the crisis had its roots in the dynamics of money, which were poorly understood by both economists and policy makers.

SILENT MONEY

There is perhaps no more graphic illustration of the inability of economists to predict a monetary crisis than the Global Financial Crisis, which began its acute phase with the 2008 failure in the US of highly leveraged hedge funds such as Bear Stearns and Lehman Brothers. In fact, this lack of clairvoyance about the crisis continued to apply even after the crisis had begun: a study by IMF economists showed the consensus of forecasters in 2008 was that not one of 77 countries considered would be in recession the next year (49 of them were).

"LEHMAN WAS NOT A BANKRUPT COMPANY."

FORMER LEHMAN BROTHERS CEO RICHARD FULD, 2015

More concerning was that, at least initially, the crisis did not seem to affect the belief in tenets such as efficient markets. In fact, it merely reinforced the notion that markets are unpredictable because they are efficient. As Fama said in 2016, "I don't think there is any concrete evidence of bubbles. A bubble to me means something that has a predictable ending. But nobody has ever been able to identify any predictability in financial markets." In 2009, another Nobel-laureate economist – Robert Lucas – noted that the unpredictable nature of markets "has been known for more than 40 years and is one of the main implications of Eugene Fama's 'efficient-market hypothesis' … If an economist had a formula that could reliably forecast crises a week in advance, say, then that formula would become part of generally available information and prices would fall a week earlier."

The usual test for a scientific theory is its ability to make accurate predictions, but with the efficient market hypothesis it seems this ability has been disabled, because any predictive failure is seen as validation. One should not conflate the efficient market hypothesis with unpredictability; if the theory did nothing more than say that markets are unpredictable, it wouldn't have been very useful. Instead, the theory proposed a specific reason for why markets are unpredictable, which is that markets correctly price assets so perturbations are due to random shocks.

As with much economic theory, the efficient market hypothesis is ultimately a statement about the relationship between price and intrinsic value, which it says are the same (at least in idealized markets). In the real economy, this question is mediated by the money system; but because efficient market theory equates price and value, there is no room for money, or the financial system as a whole. The Black–Scholes formula does not include the effects of finance, except by assuming that investors have access to credit in order to exploit anomalies.

This omission of money from the analysis meant in particular that the bubble-blowing dynamics of money creation were excluded from models. As Vítor Constâncio of the European Central Bank told his audience in a 2017 speech, "In the prevalent macro models, the financial sector was absent, considered to have a remote effect on the real economic activity … This ignored the fact that banks create money by extending credit *ex nihilo* within the limits of their capital ratio."

Finally, this absence of the financial system in the models meant that financial derivatives such as options were left out as well. This was a problem, given that – thanks in part to their cheerleaders at central banks and the IMF – they had ballooned in size to such an extent that their total liabilities represented something in the order of a quadrillion dollars, according to an estimate from the quantitative finance expert Paul Wilmott. These derivatives enabled money creation as mentioned above, but also added an extra layer of financial complexity to an already unstable system.

In other words, the main reason economists failed to predict or even understand the crisis was because their models didn't include money or credit. As discussed in the previous chapter, this lack of interest in money went back to the classical idea that money is a veil on the real economy, and was affirmed in neoclassical models which mathematicized the economy through simplification.

Ironically, another factor was that economists were highly involved in the financial system themselves. In a 2009 article, economist Barry Eichengreen described how "the occasional high-paying consulting gig" and invitations to "beachside and ski-slope retreats hosted by investment

• Above: Workers clearing their desks after the collapse of the bank Lehman Brothers.

banks" resulted in "a subconscious tendency" on the part of academic economists "to embrace the arguments of one's more 'successful' colleagues in a discipline where money, in this case earned through speaking engagements and consultancies, is the common denominator of success." A 2012 study in the *Cambridge Journal of Economics* observed that, "Perhaps these connections helped explain why few mainstream economists warned about the oncoming financial crisis."

Viewed this way, the enduring silence about money on the part of economists seems to be yet another demonstration of the power of this remarkable substance. But as any financial advisor will recommend, it is important to be able to discuss the issue of money; and since the Global Financial Crisis there has been a growing pressure to give money a more central role in economics. In the next chapter we look at how some are pressing for alternative forms of money, before turning our attention to the question of how money – and our theories about it – are currently evolving.

PART 03

FUTURE MONEY

ALTERNATIVE CURRENCIES

AS SEEN ALREADY, THE QUESTION "WHAT IS MONEY?" HAS BEEN DEBATED SINCE
THE STUFF WAS INVENTED, AND THE ANSWER OFTEN REFLECTS THE HISTORICAL
CONTEXT. FOLLOWING THE GLOBAL FINANCIAL CRISIS OF 2007–08 , INTEREST HAS
GROWN IN A VARIETY OF ALTERNATIVE CURRENCIES WHICH PROVIDE DIFFERENT AND
SOMETIMES NOVEL RESPONSES TO THIS QUESTION. THIS CHAPTER LOOKS AT SOME
SUCH ALTERNATIVES TO THE CURRENT MONETARY ORDER.

Since the founding of the Bank of England in 1694, the money system has been run as a joint public–private venture. The bank itself was founded when a private consortium lent money to the king of England, on the basis that money was needed to rebuild the Royal Navy. Today, central banks still create money by buying assets such as government bonds, which amounts to the same thing: instead of lending the government gold in return for interest payments, they purchase interest-paying bonds.

However, a few things have changed. One is that today we operate under a fiat currency system, rather than the gold standard. This makes it unclear why the government has to borrow money, when it could just create the stuff itself, as Americans once did with greenbacks.

Another change is that, when the Bank of England was founded, money creation was firmly in the hands of the state, and anyone who tried to produce counterfeit coins risked the death penalty. Today, the vast majority of money is electronically created by private banks when they make loans. It isn't counterfeit, but at the same time its production isn't directly controlled by the state. And instead of being backed by gold, the money is backed by claims on assets such as businesses or houses, which aren't quite as liquid or reliable.

As the Global Financial Crisis revealed, there has also been something of a power shift in the public–private relationship. In 1694, a consortium of private lenders set up the Bank of England because the king needed money, and was too big to fail. The amount required was £1.2 million, which was about 1.7 per cent of GDP, and about £230 million in today's money.

Three centuries later, the UK government was forced to bail out the financial sector because the banks were too big to fail but the size of the bailout announced in October 2008 was much larger, amounting to some £500 billion, or 17 per cent of GDP. Not all of these funds were tapped, but UK taxpayers have coughed up an estimated £2 billion just to keep the Royal Bank of Scotland afloat. Similar measures were employed in the US and Europe. At the time of writing, the scope of the bailout for the 2020 Cornonavirus (COVID-19) crisis has yet to be determined.

The industrialist J. Paul Getty is supposed to have said, "If you owe the bank $100, that's your problem. If you owe the bank $100 million, that's the bank's problem." Here the reverse applies: if the bank owes you £2 billion, that's your problem.

Finally, if money is based on debt, then it is also interest-bearing. That means that the money supply has to keep growing just to pay the interest. This property of the money system makes recessions worse but, as environmentalists point out, it also means that we are locked into perpetual growth which is a problem given that we live on a finite planet. It also means that money in the hands of the wealthy compounds so that they become more wealthy, which promotes inequality.

To summarize, our money system contributes to financial instability, the environmental crisis, and inequality, which are three of the main societal challenges we face today. Can we do better?

• Right: The Royal Bank of Scotland was at one point among the biggest banks in the world before becoming insolvent in 2008.

STATE MONEY

The monetary system seems to have one foot in the gold standard era, where money was treated as a finite stock of precious metal, and another foot in the modern era where money is created electronically at the press of a button. This raises a number of questions. On the one hand, as mentioned above, the state could in principle produce its own money. Recall Lincoln's argument in 1865 that: "The government should create, issue and circulate all the currency and credit needed to satisfy the spending power of the government and the buying power of the consumers." Doing so would absolve the bank of the need to pay interest on government bonds.

"THE GOVERNMENT SHOULD CREATE, ISSUE AND CIRCULATE ALL THE CURRENCY AND CREDIT"

ABRAHAM LINCOLN

The only real argument against this seems to be that it would open Pandora's box because the government might go overboard, printing too much money that could be wasted on harebrained schemes, causing inflation. As seen in recent years, however, the private sector can do a good job of printing money itself, and most of this money ends up in real estate and stock market speculation, often an unproductive use of capital that leads to asset-price inflation.

The government could even go the whole way and cut the private sector out of money creation altogether. Money would be produced by the state, and private banks could only lend what they actually had. The seignoirage from money creation would go to the state rather than the private sector. This approach, known as 100 per cent banking or full reserve banking, has been proposed over the years for varying reasons by a number of economists. One of the first was Frederick Soddy, who won the Nobel Prize for Chemistry in 1921 before turning his attention and skills to economics. In a 1927 review of Soddy's *Wealth, Virtual Wealth, and Debt*, the American economist Frank Knight wrote: "In the abstract it is absurd and monstrous for society to pay the commercial banking system interest for multiplying severalfold the quantity of the medium

of exchange when a) a public agency could do it all at negligible cost, b) there is no sense in having it done at all, since the effect is merely to raise the price level, and c) important evils result, notably the frightful instability of the whole economic system."

One disadvantage of this approach is that it would remove some of the flexibility and adaptability of the monetary system but the fact that the idea has never actually been tried on a national scale probably says more about the power of the financial sector than any technical problem with the proposal itself.

• Above: Frederick Soddy excelled in science as well as economics.

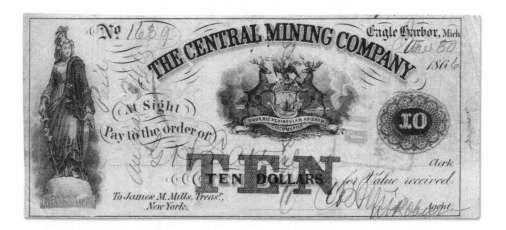

PRIVATE MONEY

Instead of the state producing its own money interest-free, and cutting out the private sector, the opposite approach would be for the government to allow a range of private currencies. The Austrian economist Friedrich von Hayek (1899–1992), who was based at the London School of Economics and later the University of Chicago, argued in his book *The Denationalization of Money* that the state should give up its "age-old prerogative of monopolizing money", which he described as "the source and root of all monetary evil". Private currencies would provide an alternative in cases where "the national monetary authorities misbehaved".

In fact, such private monies have long circulated alongside national currencies. They have often proved particularly popular during times of economic stress, when liquidity of the official currency dries up, and banks are wary of making loans. They have also usually been resisted by central banks, who wish to maintain the government monopoly on money.

During the Great Depression, local "scrip" currencies were adopted on a small scale in a number of countries. A key feature of many of these currencies was negative interest, which meant that holders had an incentive to spend the money rather than hoard it. This improved liquidity, and

• Above: During the Great Depression, local currencies, or scrips, were introduced in some places.

also helped finance the scheme. The effect was akin to that of recoinage in the Middle Ages.

In 1929, the owner of a small Bavarian coal mine, faced with closure of the mine, offered to pay his workers in a scrip which was redeemable in coal. The notes, called wara, had a monthly fee of 1 per cent which paid for the storage costs. The scheme was very successful, and was adopted by some two thousand companies from all around Germany, although the German central bank didn't like the idea and shut it down in 1931.

A similar approach was taken by the Austrian currency known as wörgl, named for the small town in the Austrian Alps where it originated in 1932. Each month, a stamp worth 1 per cent of the face value had to be applied. The town's economy thrived and attracted the attention of economists, including Irving Fisher. Mayors of 170 communities began exploring the possibility of adopting the wörgl – until in 1934 it was abruptly terminated by the Austrian National Bank.

Tauschgesellschaft: Sitz: Erfurt/Hochheim, Obmann: Hans Timm, Erfurt/Hochheim. Geschäftsstelle: Reinhard Rödiger, Berlin SO 36, Lausitzer Strasse 32, Ohne Kontroll-Prägestempel ungültig! Nachahmungen und Fälschungen sind strafbar!

16. Jan.	16. Febr.	16. März	16. April
1 Cent	1 Cent	1 Cent	1 Cent

16. Mai	16. Juni
1 Cent	1 Cent

1931

1931

16. Juli	16. August	16. Sept.	16. Okt.
1 Cent	1 Cent	1 Cent	1 Cent

16. Nov.	16. Dez.
1 Cent	1 Cent

Eine Wära = 100 Cent kostet eine RM., wenn von der Tauschgesellschaft kein anderer Preis auf Grund ihrer Richtlinien bekannt gegeben ist. Wära wird von allen Mitgliedern der Tauschgesellschaft in Zahlung genommen. Die Geschäftsstelle und die Wechselstellen der Tauschgesellschaft erheben, wenn sie Wära gegen Mark o. andere Geldsorten zurückkaufen, eine Umtauschgebühr von 1 %. Von dieser Gebühr kann Befreiung gewährt werden. An den in den Feldern bezeichneten Tagen

EINE WÄRA

TAUSCHGESELLSCHAFT

Serie B 30294

tritt ein Preisverlust von 1 % ein, falls der Verlust nicht durch Aufkleben entsprechender Centmarken auf die betreffenden Felder ausgeglichen wird. Vom 20. Dez. 1931 bis 10. Jan. 1932 wird die Wära von der Geschäftsstelle und den Wechselstellen der Tauschgesellschaft gegen Wära des Jahres 1932 kostenlos umgetauscht unter Abzug etwa fehlender Centmarken. Nach dem 10. Jan. 1932 wird dieser Schein von der Tauschgesellschaft nicht mehr angenommen.

• Above: The wara, an unofficial currency issued in Germany during the Great Depression.

• Left: Silvio Gessel's "free money", supposedly not subject to inflation or deflation.

• Below: The WIR, an unofficial Swiss currency issued during the Great Depression.

Fisher wrote a book on the subject called *Stamp Scrip*, and proposed a system for the United States where the notes should be validated with a stamp every week, for a fee of 2 per cent per week. He even suggested the slogan: "Stamp Your Scrip to Stamp Out The Depression". Again, the US government reacted by making scrips illegal in 1933.

Perhaps learning from these examples, the Swiss WIR Bank, formerly the Swiss Economic Circle, was founded in 1934 to serve small and medium-sized businesses (SMEs). Such companies often face a cashflow problem because they have to pay for supplies up front, even though their delivery horizon may be months in the future. Instead of introducing new notes, or experimenting with negative interest, the WIR system was a mutual credit network of businesses, suppliers, and clients that handled loans and eliminated the need for financial middlemen.

WIR is short for *Wirtschaftsring*, meaning economic cycle, but is also the German word for "we" which symbolizes the sense of community. The network began with 16 members and has grown to over 50,000 SMEs which amounts to about one in six Swiss companies. Not only has it avoided being shut down, it has also been widely credited with helping to stabilize the Swiss economy by providing liquidity during times of economic hardship.

LOCAL CURRENCIES

Central banks have traditionally attempted to terminate any alternative currency which poses a threat, yet interest in such currencies did not die out with the Great Depression, and there are currently thousands of local currency schemes in operation around the world. In the Canadian city of Calgary, the Calgary Dollars currency has been operating successfully since 1996, and was upgraded in 2018 with a digital app that allows users to store their money on their

> ## "I DON'T BELIEVE WE SHALL EVER HAVE GOOD MONEY AGAIN BEFORE WE TAKE THE THING OUT OF THE HANDS OF GOVERNMENT."
>
> **FRIEDRICH VON HAYEK**

CALGARY DOLLARS

phone or other device. Calgary dollars are accepted on a par with federal currency, but can't be exchanged directly.

In the English city of Bristol, a similar service is provided by the Bristol pound, which was launched in 2012, and is backed by Bristol City Council and the Bristol Credit Union. The money is accepted by a wide range of local businesses, and can also be used to pay council taxes.

The aim of such currencies is to encourage local spending, increase social capital, and improve economic resilience. Their founders often also cite the desire to use money as a way of softening some of the impacts of capitalism, favouring local supply chains and reducing the environmental impact of consumption. Calgary Dollars, for example, is run by the Arusha Centre which, according to its website, "inspires and supports communities to connect, gather, and create a socially, economically, and environmentally just future". The small scale of Calgary Dollars means that their impact is fairly minimal – which is one reason they have escaped closure.

A different kind of alternative currency is provided by corporations, where the aim is not to make you spend your money locally, but to spend your money on them. The oldest

and best-known examples are the loyalty programmes run by airlines, such as Air Miles which was launched in the UK in 1988. It was later rebranded there as Avios, but still operates as Air Miles in Canada, where it is used by an estimated two-thirds of the population. Consumers can spend their points on a variety of things, but the best deals are usually on travel – thus making Avios, in some respects, the opposite of a local currency.

Similar schemes are now run by a variety of retailers, from coffee shops to grocery stores to filling stations. While one aim is to promote customer loyalty, another advantage, from the corporation's point of view, is that they provide a vast trove of data about consumer behaviour. As money has dematerialized, it has become an increasingly important part of what author Shoshana Zuboff calls "surveillance capitalism", where what counts in a transaction is not only the actual exchange, but also the information encoded within it.

CYBERCURRENCIES

Local or corporate currencies aren't usually designed to scale up, which is one reason they are tolerated by central banks. Cybercurrencies such as Bitcoin are another thing.

The first 43,000 Bitcoins were produced or "mined" on 3 January 2009, by a person using the name Satoshi Nakamoto. To timestamp the date, he (Satoshi described himself in an online profile as male) included a headline from that day's London *Times* newspaper, reading:

• Opposite, top: The Calgary dollar is an example of a successful local currency.

• Opposite, bottom: Five Bristol Pound notes which could only be used in local, independent businesses in Bristol city.

• Right: Air Miles (or Avios) is another example of a successful alternative currency, though one with an uncertain future after the 2020 coronavirus pandemic.

"Chancellor on Brink of Second Bailout for Banks."

If the headline wasn't enough of a clue, Satoshi explained his motivation for developing the currency in a post a month later. "The root problem with conventional currency is all the trust that's required to make it work. The central bank must be trusted not to debase the currency, but the history of fiat currencies is full of breaches of that trust. Banks must be trusted to hold our money and transfer it electronically, but they lend it out in waves of credit bubbles with barely a fraction in reserve. We have to trust them with our privacy, trust them not to let identity thieves drain our accounts … With e-currency based on cryptographic proof, without the need to trust a third party middleman, money can be secure and transactions effortless."

Similar ideas had been proposed in the past, and many of Bitcoin's design elements grew out of the anarchist/cryptographic Cypherpunk movement in the 1990s, which also spawned Julian Assange's Wikileaks. In a prescient 1999 interview, the US economist Milton Friedman said, "I think that the Internet is going to be one of the major forces for reducing the role of government. And the one thing that's missing, but that will soon be developed, is a reliable e-cash, a method whereby on the Internet you can transfer funds from A to B, without A knowing B or B knowing A, the way in which I can take a 20 dollar bill and hand it over to you and there's no record of where it came from."

"BITCOIN IS THE BEGINNING OF SOMETHING GREAT: A CURRENCY WITHOUT A GOVERNMENT, SOMETHING NECESSARY AND IMPERATIVE."

NASSIM TALEB

• Above: A bitcoin "mine". Bitcoins are mined digitally, typically by powerful computer arrays.

• Opposite: Bitcoin founder, Satoshi Nakamoto.

Challenges for digital transactions include avoiding things like double-spending. One reason the music industry suffered so badly in the 1990s was that file-sharing services made it possible to send a digital copy of a song to somebody else, while keeping your own copy. If this were to happen with money, it would be great for a while, but would soon lead to chaos, because you could spend your paycheck as many times as you wanted.

The main innovation of Bitcoin was that transactions are recorded on a secure, anonymous, public ledger, known as a blockchain, which is maintained by a network of computers that make such shenanigans impossible. Unlike digital music, you can't share copies of Bitcoins with a friend, or use them multiple times. And without middlemen, transactions are faster, cheaper, and more secure.

The task of maintaining the network and verifying transactions is carried out by the "miners" who are rewarded with payments of freshly-created Bitcoins. The job is made artificially difficult by requiring miners to perform a so-called proof-of-work, which is comparable to tossing a coin millions of times (electronically, of course) until they get a certain number of heads in a row. The computing power required to do this puts a price on the blockchain and makes it economically unattractive to try tricking the system by producing a fraudulent version. While miners are located all around the world, in 2019 almost two-thirds of Bitcoin mining occurred in China, due in part to the country's low electricity costs.

THE VALUE OF BITCOIN

A common problem with alternative currencies is that it often isn't clear where their value resides. Under the gold standard, money inherited its value from precious metal, either in the coins themselves, or in notes that acted as claims on coins. Central bank currencies are created by making loans to the government, so the money is backed

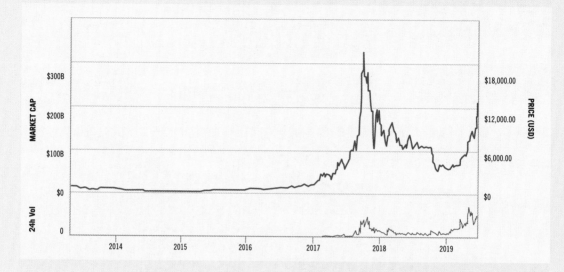

• Above: Plot showing the Bitcoin price (top, right scale), and volume (bottom) which is a measure of trading activity.

by future tax receipts, while private banks create money by loaning against real assets. In all these cases, money gets its value because it represents a debt – but alternative currencies are not usually debt-backed in the same way. So where is the value in something like Bitcoin?

Back in 2009, when Satoshi mined the first Bitcoins, their value was, of course, zero. He handed them out for free to interested parties he met online, along with a paper explaining how they could mine more coins. A community of users began to develop, and in October that year someone set up a website quoting the value of a Bitcoin as being equal to the cost of electricity required to mine a coin, which at the time was about 0.08 cents.

Once a price was available, people began to trade, as a game. Then, in May 2010, an engineer in Florida decided to see if he could actually use them to buy something real. He posted a request on the Bitcoin forum offering 10,000 Bitcoins (BTC) for two pizzas. Someone in the UK accepted the Bitcoins, and ordered the pizzas from a restaurant in Jacksonville using a credit card.

Each time a user was added, the code took slightly longer to run, so the price ticked up. And up. According to an empirical formula known as Metcalfe's Law, the worth of a network scales roughly with the number of users squared, which seems to work quite well with Bitcoin. The price is volatile, but at the time of writing a Bitcoin is worth about $6,000 (£4,800), which means those pizzas cost about $50 million. Satoshi's original 43,000 BTC "genesis block" would be worth serious cash.

Of course, for many people, this wealth is illusory, because Bitcoin doesn't meet the usual qualifications for money. It is too volatile to be a satisfactory store of wealth, or a reliable unit of account, and it hasn't caught on much with retailers, so isn't very useful as a medium of exchange. It also doesn't fit with standard ideas or theories about money. It has no link with precious metals, so bullionists don't like it, and neither can it be used to pay taxes, so it is not the same as a government-backed credit system either.

Current and former central bankers such as Alan Greenspan routinely describe the phenomenon as a "bubble", which is ironic given that they rarely applied the word to explosions in the value of real estate or stock markets under their own watch. Indeed, Bitcoin's imminent demise has been predicted many times. As Pan Gongsheng of the People's Bank of China put it in 2017, "There is only one thing left to do: sit on the river bank and see Bitcoin's body pass by one day."

While Bitcoin has certainly had its ups and downs, it does have one thing going for it, which is that – unlike most alternative currencies – it scales up to a global level, and is also very hard for central banks to shut down completely. And just because Bitcoin doesn't fit with existing ideas about money, doesn't mean that it isn't money – it might just mean that our theories need to be updated. It is backed, not by metal or taxes, but by its hard-earned and hard-working network of users. We return to this topic in the final chapter.

DIGITAL GOLD

Perhaps the best way to think about Bitcoin is as a kind of digital gold. The system was designed so that the maximum number of Bitcoins in existence does not exceed the apparently arbitrary limit of 21 million. So far, about 85 per cent of these have been mined. As with physical gold, there is, therefore, a cap on the total supply.

For comparison, according to a survey by Thomson Reuters, about 190,000 tonnes of gold have been mined throughout history. About two-thirds of that has been mined since 1950. Because gold is hard to destroy and constantly recycled, most of that gold is still being used today. If it was put all together, it would form a cube with sides of about 21 metres. According to the US Geological Survey, there are about 52,000 tonnes of minable gold still in the ground. More is likely to be discovered, but using that number suggests that we have mined nearly 80 per cent of the available gold.

As Friedman noted in 1999, cybercurrencies also have a "negative side" in that "the gangsters, the people who are engaged in illegal transactions, will also have an easier way to carry on their business." Before it was shut down in 2013, the Silk Road website, otherwise known as the "eBay for drugs", was believed to be responsible for about half of Bitcoin usage. According to the FBI, the owner of

• Above: Bitcoin has been likened to gold, in that there will only ever be a limited number of bitcoins.

• Above: Economist Milton Friedman in 1980.

Silk Road may even have attempted to arrange a hit online, paid for with Bitcoins.

Bitcoin and other cybercurrencies are also associated with a different kind of crime – hacking and cyber-theft. An early example was the collapse of the Japanese Mt Gox Bitcoin exchange in 2014, after some 850,000 Bitcoins – then worth around half a billion dollars – disappeared from its users' accounts. In 2019, Canada's largest cybercurrency exchange QuadrigaCX was closed down after the company's CEO and founder, Gerald Cotten, apparently died while on a trip in India. This was bad news for the 115,000 account holders whose funds, amounting to a quarter billion Canadian dollars, could not be accessed because it seems only Cotten held the necessary passwords. Lawyers for the customers have asked that Cotten's body be exhumed, just to make sure.

One difference between something like gold or cash is that Bitcoin is only pseudo-anonymous in the sense that, while users are anonymous, all transactions throughout the system's history are recorded in the blockchain. Regulatory bodies can, therefore, track transactions and often infer the identity of the user. So when it comes to crime, cash is still king.

NEW MONEY

Since Bitcoin was invented, it has been joined by thousands of other cybercurrencies. Some of these, such as Ethereum (whose market capitalization is about a tenth that of Bitcoin), are genuine competitors, while others are so-called scam-coins that are designed to cash in on speculator

• Above: There are hundreds if not thousands of digital currencies like Facebook's libra.

interest. The market for the latter peaked in 2017, when Bitcoin spiked to nearly $20,000.

In 2019, a new competitor was announced in the form of Facebook's Libra. At the time of writing, the currency is only in the proposal stage, but it is planned to come online in 2020. Like Bitcoin, all transactions will be recorded on a version of a blockchain. Unlike Bitcoin this will be monitored not by miners but by companies that are members of a non-profit association. Another difference is that it will be backed by a basket of major currencies, which should make the value much less volatile.

The biggest difference between Bitcoin and Libra, however, is that the former was designed as an independent, pseudo-anonymous, decentralized currency that cannot be controlled by any central bank. With Libra, all data would be owned by a consortium of corporations, which might worry anyone who is not comfortable with the idea of sharing a record of their latest transactions with Facebook, along with a complete list of all their friends.

Regulators also had a somewhat allergic reaction to Libra. French finance minister Bruno Le Maire said it is "out of the question" and US House Financial Services Committee Chair Maxine Waters quickly asked Facebook to delay launching the programme until a suitable regulatory framework was established.

The Bank of England's Mark Carney was more sympathetic, and suggested that adopting what he called a "Synthetic Hegemonic Currency" would make more sense than using one country's currency as a reserve currency, be it the US dollar or the Chinese renminbi. He thought such a currency would be best run by the public sector, and consist of a compilation of central bank digital currencies. As he told his audience in Jackson Hole, "Even a passing acquaintance with monetary history suggests that this centre won't hold. Let's end the malign neglect of the international monetary and financial system and build a system worthy of the diverse, multipolar global economy that is emerging."

The fact that society is becoming increasingly cashless means that many central banks have started to experiment with their own versions of digital currency. In Sweden, most payments are already made digitally using mobile apps, and the Swedish Riksbank is developing an e-krona. And in China, where apps such as Alipay and WeChat are popular, the People's Bank of China has been pressing ahead with development of a digital yuan, especially following the COVID-19 outbreak (digital money doesn't transmit viruses). Users can share their transaction data with the state instead of a corporation – which will be great for cutting down on crimes such as money laundering, but again no so good for privacy.

The main lesson from alternative currencies is that they are tolerated as long as they don't pose a threat to central banks. The most remarkable feature of Bitcoin is that its clever design has allowed it to survive as long as it has without being shut down. In the final chapter, we consider the remarkable hold that money of any form seems to have over the human race, and ask what modern science can teach us about its properties.

• Below: Digital payments are predicted to make paper or metal currencies redundant.

• Opposite: The Bitcoin genesis block, the first block of a block chain.

Bitcoin Genesis Block

Raw Hex Version

```
00000000   01 00 00 00 00 00 00 00   00 00 00 00 00 00 00 00   ................
00000010   00 00 00 00 00 00 00 00   00 00 00 00 00 00 00 00   ................
00000020   00 00 00 00 3B A3 ED FD   7A 7B 12 B2 7A C7 2C 3E   ....;£íýz{.²zÇ,>
00000030   67 76 8F 61 7F C8 1B C3   88 8A 51 32 3A 9F B8 AA   gv.a.È.ÃˆŠQ2:Ÿ¸ª
00000040   4B 1E 5E 4A 29 AB 5F 49   FF FF 00 1D 1D AC 2B 7C   K.^J)«_Iÿÿ...¬+|
00000050   01 01 00 00 00 01 00 00   00 00 00 00 00 00 00 00   ................
00000060   00 00 00 00 00 00 00 00   00 00 00 00 00 00 00 00   ................
00000070   00 00 00 00 00 00 FF FF   FF FF 4D 04 FF FF 00 1D   ......ÿÿÿÿM.ÿÿ..
00000080   01 04 45 54 68 65 20 54   69 6D 65 73 20 30 33 2F   ..EThe Times 03/
00000090   4A 61 6E 2F 32 30 30 39   20 43 68 61 6E 63 65 6C   Jan/2009 Chancel
000000A0   6C 6F 72 20 6F 6E 20 62   72 69 6E 6B 20 6F 66 20   lor on brink of 
000000B0   73 65 63 6F 6E 64 20 62   61 69 6C 6F 75 74 20 66   second bailout f
000000C0   6F 72 20 62 61 6E 6B 73   FF FF FF FF 01 00 F2 05   or banksÿÿÿÿ..ò.
000000D0   2A 01 00 00 00 43 41 04   67 8A FD B0 FE 55 48 27   *....CA.gŠý°þUH'
000000E0   19 67 F1 A6 71 30 B7 10   5C D6 A8 28 E0 39 09 A6   .gñ¦q0·.\Ö¨(à9.¦
000000F0   79 62 E0 EA 1F 61 DE B6   49 F6 BC 3F 4C EF 38 C4   ybàê.aÞ¶Iö¼?Lï8Ä
00000100   F3 55 04 E5 1E C1 12 DE   5C 38 4D F7 BA 0B 8D 57   óU.å.Á.Þ\8M÷º..W
00000110   8A 4C 70 2B 6B F1 1D 5F   AC 00 00 00 00            ŠLp+kñ._¬....
```

OF MIND AND MONEY

THROUGHOUT ITS LONG HISTORY, MONEY HAS TAKEN ON MANY SHAPES, FROM COINS MADE OF ELECTRUM, TO BITCOINS MADE OF ELECTRONS. DESPITE THESE CHANGES TO ITS EXTERNAL FORM, MONEY HAS REMAINED ENDLESSLY FASCINATING AND ELUSIVE, AS IF THERE IS SOMETHING INTRINSIC ABOUT ITS NATURE THAT CAPTURES AND ENTRANCES THE HUMAN MIND.

At the same time, as if unsettled by its power, our economic theories have insisted on treating money as a dull and lifeless medium of exchange, of no special interest in itself. In recent years, that has finally started to change as economists have incorporated a little more human emotion into their models – and shed some light on what quality it is that makes money such powerful stuff.

• Below: Behavioural economist Daniel Kahneman argued that we fear losses more than we value gains.

BEHAVIOURAL ECONOMICS

The field of behavioural economics goes back to early research performed by two Israeli psychologists, Daniel Kahneman and Amos Tversky. Using their university students as guinea pigs, they performed a number of experiments showing that, when it comes to economic decision making, we often do not conform closely to the ideal of "rational economic man". Instead, we exhibit numerous cognitive biases which tend to skew our thinking.

• Above: A copy of international bestseller Thinking, Fast and Slow by Nobel Laureate Daniel Kahneman.

Many of the key ideas from behavioural economics could be summed up in a single diagram showing a so-called value function. The horizontal axis shows losses or gains, which correspond to amounts of money, while the vertical axis shows the perceived value. In neoclassical economics, the value is just the expected utility. Kahneman and Tversky's version differs in a number of respects.

One feature of their graph is that value tends to grow more slowly as the financial gain increases. This corresponds to the "law of diminishing returns" which means that increasing net worth by £100 sparks less joy for a millionaire than it does for a poor person.

Another feature is that the graph is asymmetric around the origin. In particular, the slope of the line is steeper for losses than it is for gains. This reflects the empirical fact that people are "loss averse" in the sense that they are roughly twice as sensitive to losses as they are to gains. Investors

may feel mildly pleased if their investments increase by 10 per cent in a year, but call their broker in a panic if they drop by the same amount.

Finally, losses and gains are measured relative to a central reference point. This is where it gets tricky, because it turns out that the reference point is highly dependent on context, and the particular "mental account" being used.

As an example, imagine that you show up at a cinema, but when you reach into your pocket for the cash to buy a ticket you discover that the £10 note you were keeping there must have fallen out, perhaps while you were taking out your keys. Would you still go ahead and buy a ticket anyway? In a survey by Kahneman and Tversky, 88 per cent said yes.

Now, suppose instead that you had already bought a ticket, but this time when you reached into your pocket it wasn't there. Would you still buy another ticket in this case? In the original survey, only 44 per cent said they

would. The reason, according to Kahneman and Tversky, is that we hold the two sums in different mental accounts, with different reference levels. The cash belongs to a large fund for miscellaneous expenses, so £10 is relatively small change. The ticket, however, belongs to a more specific fund for watching movies. Buying a second ticket is mentally equivalent to paying twice as much to see a movie, which is hard to do, even if in numerical terms it represents the same loss of £10 as misplacing the cash.

This kind of "mental accounting" also explains why we find it easy to spend something like a gift card given to us by a friend. We experience it as an unexpected windfall to be enjoyed, rather than just more money which should be applied to something boring like a utility bill. In traditional theory, money is a neutral medium of exchange, but in practice the context is important.

• Above: Kahneman and Tversky argue that consumers do not generally conform to the ideal of the "rational economic man".

• Opposite (top): Kahneman and Tversky used the analogy of losing money for a cinema ticket to explain behavioural economics.

• Opposite: "Mental accounting" can often have unforeseen affects on your personal finances' bottom line.

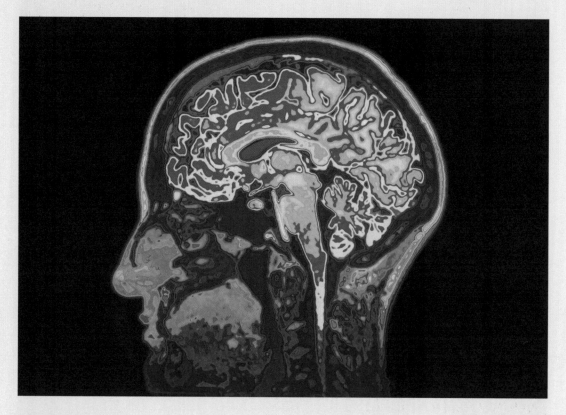

NEUROECONOMICS

The view of money as a neutral substance also belies its effects on the human brain. The findings of behavioural economics have been complemented by the new field of neuroeconomics, which combines the disciplines of neuroscience and economics to study how people make financial decisions.

Stanford University neuroscientist Brian Knutson carried out a series of experiments where subjects were offered amounts of cash while they were in a machine having their brain scanned. He found that the opportunity to make easy money created a surge of the neurotransmitter dopamine in a small area of the brain called the nucleus accumbens, which is known to play a central role in the neural circuitry of drug addiction.

Money was such a powerful stimulant that, according to Knutson, it overwhelmed nearly everything else. "Nothing had an effect on people like money – not naked bodies, not corpses. It got people riled up. Like food provides motivation for dogs, money provides it for people." According to traditional theory, money is just a neutral

medium of exchange, so obtaining money should not, in itself, be a source of great pleasure, especially if the amounts are small compared to what one already has. But the scanning research vividly illustrated the fact that we get immediate pain and pleasure from the prospects of losing or gaining money.

In another experiment, published in 2005, neuroscientists at Caltech gave subjects a choice between two decks of cards. One, they were told, consisted of ten red and ten blue cards, while the other had an unknown mix of red and blue. If they could correctly guess the colour of a single card drawn from the pack, then they would win a prize of $10.

In either case, the odds of winning are 50-50. With the second deck, the subject doesn't know the mix of cards, but that doesn't matter because they are all either red or blue.

So, in theory, the two decks should be treated the same way. However, the results showed that people were far more likely to choose the deck with the known mix. The reason, it seemed, was that they were using a different part of the brain for the case where the mix was uncertain. Patients who'd had that area of the brain damaged by stroke didn't show the same bias. This "ambiguity aversion" has been proposed as an explanation for why investors tend to have a home-country bias – they prefer to invest in stocks where they feel they know the odds, rather than take a punt on the unknown.

As the resolution of brain scanners improves, researchers can tease out more detail. One paper, published in 2018, compared the brain's reaction to monetary and humorous rewards. The latter involved looking at cartoons, which had been selected off the internet by a group of humour research experts to make sure they were funny. The punchline of the paper was that the brain's response to getting money and getting a joke are similar in that they each involve the phases of anticipation and reward, but the anticipation of a monetary payment had more of an effect on the nucleus accumbens, which may explain why we can become addicted to money but not to cartoons.

THE PSYCHOLOGY OF MONEY

Of course, psychologists have long known that money holds enormous pull over the human psyche – including their own. In a letter to a colleague, Sigmund Freud wrote that, "My mood also depends very strongly on my earnings. Money is laughing gas for me." Freud associated money with the anal stage of development, claiming in one of his works that whether it be "in the ancient civilization, in myths, fairy tales, and superstitions, in unconscious thinking, in dreams and in neuroses … money is brought into the most intimate relationship with dirt."

The Jungian psychologist James Hillman, meanwhile, said that money corresponds to a hidden form of psychic energy. "To find the soul of modern man or woman, begin by searching into those irreducible embarrassing facts of the money complex, that crazy crab scuttling across the floors of silent seas." According to psychiatrist David Krueger, "Money is probably the most emotionally meaningful object in contemporary life. Only food and sex are its close competitors as common carriers of such strong, diverse feelings, significances, and strivings." It is unsurprising

"MY MOOD ALSO DEPENDS VERY STRONGLY ON MY EARNINGS. MONEY IS LAUGHING GAS FOR ME"

SIGMUND FREUD

• Above: How do we make choices when confronted with apparently similar products.

that money is also associated with a range of psychological pathologies, ranging from compulsive bargain hunting to compulsive gambling, and is a frequent cause of marital and family conflict.

Behavioural economics shows that we depart in many ways from the economic model of rational man, but in one respect money and wealth do align us more closely with that model, by making us behave in a more selfish, less altruistic way. The US psychologist Paul Piff calls it the "asshole effect". Even mentioning the word "money" has been shown to prompt people to act in a less ethical manner. As discussed in the previous chapters, some alternative currencies work to calm this effect, notably by encouraging local interactions.

The fact that money is much more than a neutral medium of exchange also means that we are sensitive to things like form and presentation. Just as monetary rewards create a sensation of pleasure, so the act of payment creates a sensation of pain. As with other kinds of pain, this "pain of paying" is useful in that it acts as a kind of internal warning bell, without which we might find ourselves

spending too much. This pain tends to be lower when a transaction is smooth, seamless, and abstract – as when we tap a card at a store – than when it involves counting out hard-earned coins.

In one 2001 study, researchers at MIT set up an auction for students to buy tickets to professional sports events (a basketball game and a baseball game). Some of the students were instructed that payment had to be in cash, and they needed to have "ready access to a local cash machine". Others were told that payment was by credit card, and they needed to specify which kind of card they would use. The results showed that people were willing to pay almost twice as much using the credit card.

Similar results have been obtained by a number of other studies, including imaging experiments that showed how the act of deciding to make a purchase activates brain circuits associated with affective pain – the feelings of unpleasantness that we get when we contemplate some undesirable future event. The effect was far lower for credit than for cash. Amazon has been experimenting with a number of Amazon Go convenience stores where customers don't even need to produce a card. Instead, they scan their phone on entry to identify their Amazon account, pick up what they want, and walk out. Cameras track their motion through the store, register what they take, and charge the purchases to their account.

The fact that money is becoming increasingly virtual and abstract, and payment increasingly pain-free and frictionless, may be one reason (along with low interest rates) that consumer debt in many countries is at unprecedented levels.

HOW MUCH

Behavioural economics and neuroscience can help us understand many areas of finance. Loss aversion, for example, explains why investors tend to hold on to poorly performing stocks – it might make more sense to sell them, but that would mean acknowledging the loss. An easy way to improve your savings rate is to set up an automatic deduction each month – if you don't see the money in your current account, then you don't experience any loss of pleasure by "losing" it to your savings.

"A PERSON WHO HAS NOT MADE PEACE WITH HIS LOSSES IS LIKELY TO ACCEPT GAMBLES THAT WOULD BE UNACCEPTABLE TO HIM OTHERWISE."

DANIEL KAHNEMAN

At the same time, critics argue that much of this comes down to common sense – you don't need a brain scanner to know that paying for something in cash can be a painful experience. And when it comes to major issues such as how economists build macroeconomic models, behavioural economics is best seen as a relatively minor adjustment to the neoclassical approach that has so far had little impact on mainstream economics. The reason, as we have already seen, is rather simple: mainstream models don't properly include money in the first place.

• Above: John Maynard Keynes described the fundamentally indeterminate nature of money.

The emotionally volatile nature of money means that it doesn't fit easily with economic models that assume rationality but it also has a number of other properties that elude the traditional approach. Conventional models are based on the idea that change is smooth and continuous but the creation or transfer of money is an instantaneous process. When you tap your card at a store, the money doesn't drain out in a flow, it just jumps. The same is true when a bank creates new money by issuing a loan.

Money and debt also create financial entanglements by linking debtors and creditors. In conventional economics, people and firms are represented in aggregate, so if one person loans money to another then the net effect is zero. As economist Paul Krugman put it, in capital letters, in 2019: "DEBT IS MONEY WE OWE TO OURSELVES." But this is like saying that theft is money we steal from ourselves. One reason financial derivatives – which represent a kind

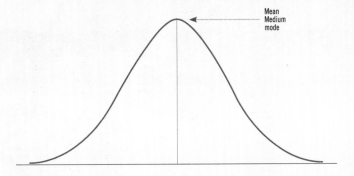

Mean
Medium
mode

• Opposite: Einstein helped start a revolution in physics. Many believe that one is overdue in economics.

• Above: The bell-curve graph depicts normal distribution with the top of the course showing the mean, mode and median of the data collected.

"DEBT IS MONEY WE OWE TO OURSELVES."

PAUL KRUGMAN

of super-entanglement of the global financial system – have been allowed to grow so large is because of this attitude that debt doesn't matter. This tends to be sorely tested whenever there is a crisis and someone decides not to pay (see the COVID-19 crisis).

As we have seen, money is fundamentally dualistic in that it combines the real properties of an owned object, with the virtual properties of number, which is why it can take the form of solid things such as coins, or of virtual money transfers. These dualistic properties, combining ownership and calculation, are what make it such a psychologically active substance. And prices in the economy are fundamentally indeterminate until measured through transactions.

To summarize, money is created and transmitted in discrete parcels, it entangles its users, it is dualistic, and prices are indeterminate. As John Maynard Keynes wrote in 1926, "We are faced at every turn with the problems of Organic Unity, of Discreteness, of Discontinuity – the whole is not equal to the sum of the parts, comparisons of quantity fail us, small changes produce large effects, the assumptions of a uniform and homogeneous continuum are not satisfied."

Keynes' comments were a reaction in part to contemporary developments in physics – he met Einstein, and the title of his *General Theory of Employment, Interest and Money* was inspired by Einstein's *General Theory of*

Relativity. A growing number of researchers are coming to the conclusion that the money system might have more in common with non-mechanistic physics than previously thought. In particular, it turns out that the mathematical methodology of quantum mechanics (the word quantum is from the Latin for "how much") can be usefully applied to modelling both mental processes of the sort studied in behavioural economics, and financial transactions.

For example, if you decide to put your house up for sale, then you can suggest a price, but the real price is only known once someone actually buys it, with the purchase acting as a measurement procedure. In quantum economics, the house price is modelled using a probabilistic wave function, which specifies only the probability that the house will be sold for a range of prices. The wave function then "collapses" to a single price when measured. This is the same as in quantum physics, where the position of a particle is specified by a wave function that only collapses when measured in an experiment.

Similarly, mental states can be modelled using wave functions which collapse to a particular state when a choice is made. As computer scientist Scott Aaronson points out, quantum mathematics is "about information and probabilities and observables, and how they relate to each other". And it applies as much to financial interactions as it does to subatomic ones.

THE ELIXIR OF ETERNAL GROWTH

The idea that money can be modelled using the tools of quantum mathematics does not imply that money is somehow the same as a subatomic particle any more than modelling the economy using Newtonian equations, as has been done for centuries, implies that money is the same as a planetary object. But it may help shed light on some of money's confounding properties.

As we have seen in this brief history, money is not something that emerged by accident, but is best seen as a kind of designed social technology, that requires a great deal of work and coordination in order to succeed – whether that work is performed by temple bureaucrats enforcing payments in ancient Sumeria; armies forcing slaves to mine gold in ancient Greece and Rome; kings imposing debts on their subjects in medieval Europe; the United States backing its global reserve currency with its massive army in the 20th century; or energy-hungry Bitcoin miners in the 21st.

Despite the fact that we designed the stuff, we seem very poor at understanding how it actually works.

• Above: Housing prices are modelled according probabilistic wave function, which specifies only the probability that the house will be sold for a range of prices.

• Below Money is dynamically linked to economic transactions, which are themselves the source of economic growth.

Economists spent years building mathematical models that excluded it from their analysis, until more recently gingerly attempting to put it back in through areas such as behavioural economics.

Money has traditionally been seen as an elixir of economic growth – and when growth was seen as unconstrained, we could perhaps afford to turn a blind eye to its dynamics. We are currently at a turning point, however, where economic growth is too often directly at odds with environmental limits and the desire for social fairness and stability.

Since its invention, and through the multiple twists and turns of its long history, money has been at the centre of the human experience. The future of this remarkable substance promises to be just as interesting.

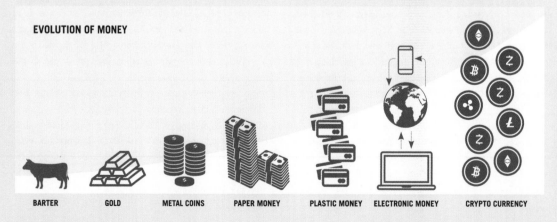

EVOLUTION OF MONEY

BARTER   GOLD   METAL COINS   PAPER MONEY   PLASTIC MONEY   ELECTRONIC MONEY   CRYPTO CURRENCY

POSTFACE: PANDEMIC

The Covid-19 pandemic of early 2020 caused the wealthy economies to react in a historically unprecedented way. State-imposed "social distancing" measures of varying severity designed to slow the spread of the SARS CoV-2 virus were enacted, which triggered a massive slow-down in economic activity. After just 6-8 weeks of aggressive lockdowns, US unemployment had soared to levels not seen since the Great Depression, the British economy was facing its biggest annual contraction since 1706 according to the Bank of England, and the United Nations estimated that up to half of global livelihoods were under threat.

The monetary and fiscal tools employed to contain the damage from state-induced deflation were almost as startling and, at the time of writing, difficult to quantify. The UK committed at least £330 billion to emergency business loans and paycheque protection; the US Congress appropriated some $3.3 trillion for similar measures; and by May 2020 it was estimated that the total cost of the global bailouts could top $10 trillion.

Yet at the time of writing it is far from clear whether these, or any measures, will be enough to prevent a second Great Depression. If the 1930s version was exacerbated by government restrictions in the money supply, the current crisis is characterized by collapsing demand which may well be beyond the scope of all fiscal and monetary tools. And while the state can create money and boost asset prices by pressing a button, restarting the economy is another thing. Extra cash will not be spent in businesses that are closed by government order, or that are kept from flourishing by public fear.

While in early 2020 it is far too early to draw any detailed lessons from the Covid-19 experience, the crisis has certainly exposed the lack of resilience in the economic and financial systems of even the richest countries. Failing to build up emergency reserves in terms of personal finance, investment strategy and health policy is a bit like living in a home without insurance – cheap, and then very expensive. Our economy system is based on optimising efficiency, but a basic lesson from natural systems is that what counts in the long run is not so much efficiency, but robustness (which is why for example our bodies have two kidneys).

The crisis has also further exposed deep social and financial inequalities – viruses might be agnostic to things

• Below: The New York Stock Exchange faced massive uncertainty at the onset of the COVID-19 pandemic.

like social class, but risk is not so evenly distributed. Social distance is easier to maintain on a secluded country estate, or for that matter a plutocrat's luxury underground bunker, than on a crowded bus or assembly line.

Putting the economy on pause has also exposed something else – we won't quickly forget how it looks to see streets free of traffic and the sky free of contrails, breathe clean air, and feel the planet enjoying a brief respite from the ecological onslaught known as the anthropocene.

And regarding the central topic of this book, the crisis has only emphasised both the importance and the two-sided nature of money. Just as a fish (probably) doesn't think much about water until it is beached, so money looms somewhat larger in our collective consciousness when people suddenly stop paying bills. At the same time, the crisis has reinforced the notion that money – and the financial system as a whole – is a virtual creation, that is subject to political and financial manipulations, and whose

link to real economic activity is complex and sometimes counter-intuitive. This was illustrated by the April 30 headline "U.S. Stocks Have Their Best Month Since 1987" even as measures such as employment and GDP collapsed.

The crisis has also proved that if money is a metric, it is better at measuring power than usefulness, since the overlap between "essential workers" such as nurses who keep society working, and the wealthy or highly-paid who extract the greatest gains, has been revealed as small. One thing that seems certain is that the pandemic will take its place in future histories as another in a long line of social and financial events that has shaped, influenced or revised our approach to money.

• Opposite: Opposite: Piccadilly Circus, London, deserted during lockdown.

• Below: Protestors demonstrate against stay-at-home orders in Denver, Colorado in April 2020.

FURTHER READING

George Akerlof and Robert Shiller, *Phishing for Phools: The Economics of Manipulation and Deception*, Princeton University Press, 2015

Peter Bernstein, *The Power of Gold: The History of an Obsession*, John Wiley & Sons, 2000

Catherine Eagleton and Jonathan Williams, *Money: A History*, Firefly Books, 2007

William Stanley Jevons, *Letters and Journal of W. Stanley Jevons*, edited by Harriet A. Jevons Macmillan, 1886

John Kenneth Galbraith, *Money: Whence It Came, Where It Went*, Houghton Miflin, 1975

Charles Kindleberger, *A Financial History of Western Europe*, HaperCollins, 1984

Daniel Kahneman, *Thinking, Fast and Slow*, Farrar, Straus & Giroux, 2011

Jacques Le Goff, *Money and the Middle Ages*, Polity Press, 2012

Satoshi Nakamoto, "Bitcoin: A Peer-to-Peer Electronic Cash System", https://bitcoin.org/bitcoin.pdf

David Orrell, *Quantum Economics: The New Science of Money*, Icon Books, 2018

Tomas Sedlacek, *Economics of Good and Evil: The Quest for Economic Meaning from Gilgamesh to Wall Street*, Oxford University Press, 2011

Jack Weatherford, *The History of Money Crown*, Three Rivers Press, 1997

Carl Wennerlind, *Casualties of Credit: The English Financial Revolution, 1620–1720*, Harvard University Press, 2011

INDEX

CREDITS